MANAGEMENT DEVELOPMENT:
DESIGN, EVALUATION, AND
IMPLEMENTATION

MANAGEMENT DEVELOPMENT:
DESIGN, EVALUATION, AND IMPLEMENTATION

by

Robert J. House, Ph.D.

Executive Director,
McKinsey Foundation for Management Research, Inc.
Associate Professor
Bernard M. Baruch School of Business
and Public Administration

contributors:

Henry L. Tosi, Jr., Ph.D.
Assistant Professor
University of Maryland

John R. Rizzo, Ph.D.
Assistant Professor
The George Washington University

Richard C. Dunnock
Corporate Manager
Philco Corporation

BUREAU OF INDUSTRIAL RELATIONS
Graduate School of Business Administration
The University of Michigan
Ann Arbor

To three contributors to the
good life: B.B.B.

FOREWORD

When Dr. House was a member of the faculty of the Ohio State University, he spent one semester at the Bureau of Industrial Relations at the University of Michigan doing library research into studies which purported to measure the effects of management development. He dug deep, finding several hundred "rigorously" conducted researches into the subject. Having found these, he arrayed them for common threads which might indicate what makes management development succeed or fail. This led him to his commitment approach, which is actually a compendium of all of the behavioral research on the effects of systematic efforts to change managerial behavior through conscious and planned efforts. Subsequent field tests of the theory have been most heartening.

Dr. House's theory of management development has been presented to hundreds of managers in the BIR seminar Management by Objectives and has withstood the tests of challenges from practical managers. Later, as a member of the Bureau staff, the author conducted seminars on the subject of his research and discussed his findings fully with management development men. Its reception and application have been widespread.

This book is a summary of Dr. House's own investigations, plus that of several of his colleagues and collaborators. It all reflects his empirical studies in numerous firms for which he has served as a consultant. The strongest impetus for this book was Dr. House's monograph, published by the Bureau of Industrial Relations in 1961, entitled "A Predictive Theory of Management Development." The monograph was so well received by both the business and academic communities that the author spent considerably more time and effort in further research and writing. The final product represents a most authoritative theory of why management development efforts fail in so many situations: the failure to isolate, quantify, measure, and

5

study the variables of the dynamic process of education and development.

Appreciation is due to Mr. Thomas S. Roberts of the BIR for his assistance in research with Dr. House. Beatrice Schrader and Elizabeth Sumner edited the manuscript; Pamela Gilson did the proofing. Mr. William H. Price coordinated the editorial efforts and carries the final responsibility for the editorial content of the book.

This book, describing the type of management development taught and practiced at Michigan, will have a very significant impact on management training in the 1960's and beyond.

GEORGE S. ODIORNE, *Director*
Bureau of Industrial Relations
Ann Arbor, Michigan, 1967

CONTENTS

CHAPTER 1

MANAGEMENT DEVELOPMENT:
WHAT, HOW, WHY?
by Robert J. House

According to a recent *Wall Street Journal* article,[1] U.S. companies, in an effort to fight the increasing problem of management obsolescence, put some 500,000 executives through on-the-job training courses, management seminars, and formal academic programs during 1966 alone—nearly twice the number put through such programs in 1961. In 1953 only four universities offered programs specifically conceived and directed for executives, whereas today more than forty universities offer advanced management training programs, ranging in duration from several weeks to several months.

Despite this increasing effort on the part of industry and educational institutions to turn out effective managers for all industries, "there is a world-wide shortage of qualified managers and technicians...(which is) impeding company development and slowing national growth."[2] Not only is industry failing to develop adequate numbers of managers quickly enough, it also fails in understanding precisely why. Note the following contradictory opinions, for example, frequently expressed by managerial groups at various organizational levels as to why management development efforts fail:

"This training and development stuff is all good, but it's my boss who really needs it."
— middle and lower level managers

---

[1] T. Bray, "Obsolete Executives," *Wall Street Journal*, January 24, 1966, 1.
[2] K. K. Bivens, J. Greene, and G. C. Thompson, "Identifying and Developing Managers—World-Wide Shortages and Remedies," *The Conference Board Record*, Vol. 2, No. 6 (June 1965), 23.

"If top management would only show active support of the program, it would be a certain success."
                              — the staff specialist
"Management development? Active support? Why, I'm doing that all the time."
                              — top management

Such comments as those above illustrate an all too common phenomenon in business and industrial training: that frequently only lower level managers are trained, while their superiors are not even prepared to accept change. This criticism is valid as far as it goes. It does not, however, provide a complete explanation for the failure of industry to develop managers fast enough.

Perhaps more pertinent to the problems is a comment by Levy, who, in reviewing a recent survey of management development practices, states that "the major issue...is to recognize that we are still primarily talking about an art rather than the making of scientific statements....Very few studies have systematically evaluated the impact of these different practices. To the extent this continues, management devopment will continue to be an art rather than a science or an applied technology."[3]

How, then, might this problem of management development be more systematically evaluated and alleviated? Such is the purpose and scope of this book, which represents one attempt to illuminate problems of management development by means of social science investigations and findings related to behavioral change.

What is advanced in these chapters is based upon 1) actual experiences with management development efforts reported in the social science and business literature since 1948 (the approximate date when industry began planned efforts to develop managers), and 2) social science findings resulting from studies which deal with important aspects of the development process, such as changing attitudes, transferring training from learning to job situations, and overcoming resistance to change. We have confined our analysis to social science studies or reports

---

[3] S. Levy, *Personnel Psychology*, Vol. 18, No. 1 (Spring 1965), 127.

of company experiences which meet the minimum requirements of social science research: studies which provide for
isolation, observation, and measurement of the variables under
study.

Of the 200 studies found meeting these minimum requirements, approximately 135 deal not only with the effect of
development efforts on individuals or organizations, but also
with the conditions under which development efforts are likely
to be successful or not.[4] Such studies clearly demonstrate that
if development is to be successful, it must be geared not only to
the participant's needs and learning abilities, but also to the
particular requirements and practices of the organization in
which he manages. When development has not been based on
these considerations, it fails to effectively influence either managerial performance or major operational problems. Consider
the following two reports which illustrate how management
development efforts have actually created rather than solved
problems:

1) In 1962, a British manufacturing company employed an
outside consultant to conduct a management training
program for 97 office and plant supervisors. The overall
program objective was to increase the general efficiency
of the company. Some of the specific areas covered were
methods improvement, planning and controlling work,
human relations, and estimating and purchasing. As a result of the program, the supervisors recognized that
changes had to be initiated by top management in order
for the participants to function effectively. When it became apparent that the necessary changes were not going
to be made, those who had participated in the program
began to seek other employment. Within a year after the
course, 19 of the supervisors had left the company. Of
these 19, 12 reported that the course had precipitated
their decision. An additional 25 had applied for jobs outside the firm; of these 25, 15 said that the course had
been the basis of these applications. 83 supervisors said

---

4 See Appendix 1 for a rather technical review of these studies and the conceptual framework inferred from them.

that the course was a failure because it failed to change the behavior of top management.[5]

2) A study conducted at the International Harvester Company in 1955 indicated that management development courses frequently result in conflict between the manager and his immediate superior when the superior does not practice the principles which the subordinate manager has been taught in a management development course.[6]

Reasons for Disappointing Results

These examples show that development programs are too often given only to one level of management. Social science literature suggests several other reasons for the disappointing results. Namely:

1) Development is a long-term process which requires extensive lead time and planning. Few efforts to date have recognized this requirement. Most have expected startling results from a few weeks of training or from a single development technique. (See Chapter 2.)

2) Too few development programs include operational specifications of how participants' behavior and, through this, organizational results are expected to change as a result of the program. (Chapter 2 discusses setting precise objectives.)

3) Because of lack of understanding of the importance of the logical sequence involved in improving operational performance (the ultimate objective of development), individuals and firms often have attempted to circumvent one or more tasks. (This task sequence is described later in this chapter.)

4) In those programs for which specific terminal behavior has been indicated, the variables all too infrequently are analyzed according to the quantity, quality, and complex interaction required to achieve this terminal behavior. Some variables crucial to the implementation of change are informal group norms; formal organizational policy;

---

[5] A. J. M. Sykes, "The Effect of a Supervisory Training Course in Changing Supervisors' Perceptions and Expectations of the Role of Management," *Human Relations*, Vol. 15, No. 3 (August 1962), 227-243.

[6] E. A. Fleishman, E. F. Harris, and H. E. Burtt, *Leadership and Supervision in Industry: An Evaluation of a Supervisory Training Program* (Columbus, Ohio: The Ohio State University, 1955).

attitude of participants' superiors toward change; and
the existence of such incentives as increased pay and
promotions. (See Chapter 3.)

5) Where support from superiors or from company policies
is not available, the participant must compensate for this
by sound judgment, ability, and a strong personal wish
to develop. He also must have the respect of his associates
and subordinates. Since such people are the exception,
and since organizations rarely provide all the necessary
environmental support, the failure of management development programs to change organizational performance is not surprising.

If development attempts fail, there are two alternatives:
1) abandon the program, or 2) examine the reasons for its
failure, make indicated changes, and try again. Assuming that
there was a logical basis for the initial favor with which development efforts were welcomed, this book attempts to
examine the reasons listed above for their failure and to suggest changes which should assist the manager in planning,
implementing, and evaluating management development
efforts for himself, his subordinates, and his organization.

Management Development and the Developmental Process

For purposes of this book, *management development* is defined as any attempt to improve current or future managerial
performance by imparting information, conditioning attitudes,
or increasing skills. Hence, management development includes
such efforts as on-the-job coaching, counseling, classroom
training, job rotation, selected readings, planned experience,
and assignment to understudy positions. Attempts to change
individual performance have very limited application. What is
needed are concepts and methods which treat simultaneously
the individual and the environment in which he works, rather
than more refined methods for individual learning.

For ease of understanding, the *developmental process* will
be described in two ways: first, we will consider the major
changes involved in the developmental process over a period
of time; we will then turn to the question of how this change
is encouraged or discouraged by superiors, peers, and the company's formal organizational system.

Time Sequence of Changes

The process of development generally consists of five changes which occur over a period of time:[7]

1) The manager increases his level of information by reading, listening, and observing. This stage requires that he be provided with reading matter or lectures relevant to his developmental goals, or that he be placed in work situations which provide examples of new practices.

2) He then reflects upon the various concepts and practices he has learned, considers his earlier convictions, and develops attitudes toward the new concepts and practices just learned. In helping the manager develop attitudes conducive to behavior change, it is often useful to provide each participant in a management development effort an opportunity to discuss with other participants both the validity and potential applicability of the information and new concepts presented.

3) As the manager practices applying the new techniques, either during training or on the job, his developing knowledge is translated into skills. The participant should generally receive sufficient practice opportunities so that he can eliminate inefficient behavior and become competent in the application of the new skills *before* he is required to act independently on his job.

4) On the job he works within the previously established management practices. The policies of top management, the practices of his immediate boss, and the behavior of job associates constitute the most influential aspects of the environment. If these are consistent with the practices taught in the learning phase of the development program, the participant will be allowed to apply his new knowledge and skills to actual job situations. Performance change at this point requires coaching or counseling from an immediate superior. The instruction process now must be assumed by a line manager, rather than a staff person or through the use of a textbook.

---

[7] It is not claimed that this is the only valid sequence or that it is a necessary one. (See p. 17 for a discussion of this issue.)

5) The changed job performance of individual managers will result in improved organizational performance when it is coordinated with that of others in the development program toward specified organizational goals.

Variables Influencing Change

Having discussed the change-through-development process, we can now turn our attention to the specific variables which influence the process. The major factors include: 1) the manager being trained, 2) his superiors, 3) his peers, and 4) the formal organizational system.

The manager's ability to learn. Participant learning ability is a necessary prerequisite for accomplishing management development objectives. However, since most development programs do not include subject matter of highly complex or abstract nature, and since most managers have been found in earlier research to have above average scholastic ability and intelligence,[8] learning ability does not usually present a problem. However, where the development effort requires learning at a rapid pace, or where the subject matter is highly complex (such as probability theory or sophisticated mathematical techniques), managers should be selected on the basis of their ability to assimilate and understand the information presented in the learning phase of the development effort. Studies by Neel and Dunn,[9] Savitt,[10] Mahoney, Jerdee, and Nash,[11] Gruenfeld,[12] Katzell,[13] and Thistlethwaite, DeHann, and Kamenet-

[8] R. M. Stogdill, "Personal Factors Associated with Leadership: A Survey of the Literature," *Journal of Psychology*, Vol. 25 (1948), 35-71.

[9] R. G. Neel and R. E. Dunn, "Predicting Success in Supervisory Training Programs by the Use of Psychological Tests," *Journal of Applied Psychology*, Vol. 44, No. 5 (October 1960), 358-360, especially 360.

[10] M. A. Savitt, "Is Management Training Worthwhile?" *Personnel*, Vol. 34, No. 2 (September-October 1957), 79-82.

[11] T. A. Mahoney, T. H. Jerdee, and A. N. Nash, "Predicting Managerial Effectiveness," *Personnel Psychology*, Vol. 13, No. 2 (Summer 1960), 147-163.

[12] L. W. Gruenfeld, "Selection of Executives for a Training Program," *Personnel Psychology*, Vol. 14, No. 4 (Winter 1960), 421-431.

[13] R. A. Katzell, "Testing a Training Program in Human Relations," *Personnel Psychology*, Vol. 1, No. 3 (Autumn 1948), 319-329.

zky,[14] indicate that various measures of learning ability are positively related to the effect of management development.

Attitudes and skills of supervisors. Without awareness that development means change in managerial performance, many managers have participated in or encouraged their subordinates to participate in development efforts only to find that they really prefer the status quo. To be conceptually meaningful, development must be defined in terms of the specific changes that are desired. The manager who says, "I want management development," implies that he is seeking a change either in himself, in his subordinates, or in some part, if not in all, of his organization. Frequently, however, a manager makes such statements without being aware that his own attitudes and performance frequently thwart subordinates' attempts to bring about the implied change. To prevent this, managers must determine whether the changes that a development program attempts to effect are acceptable not only to him but are also compatible with prevailing organizational practices.

Immediate associates. In addition to the manager's supervisor, there is the informal organization composed of the participant's peers and associates who exert social influence over him. This influence is a combination of 1) informal expectations of the members of the organization, 2) precedents, and 3) tradition. The informal organization is expressed implicitly in the form of group norms, values, and informal activities. Informal group values may include attitudes toward discipline and punishment, priorities placed on different types of work, or belief in a particular kind of management behavior.

The formal authority system. This system consists of the work environment and the surrounding elements resulting from top management philosophy, policies, decisions, and legal precedent; the organization structure; and the formal system of control. The formal authority system is usually expressed in the form of written objectives, policies, job descriptions, procedures, standards of performance, formal appraisal sys-

---

14 D. L. Thistlethwaite, H. de Haan, and J. Kamenetzky, "The Effects of 'Directive' and 'Nondirective' Communication Procedures on Attitudes," *Journal of Abnormal and Social Psychology*, Vol. 51, No. 1, (July 1955), 107-113, especially 110.

tems, formal incentives, and compensation systems. Before
starting a development program, it is advisable to ascertain
that the behavior prescribed in the learning effort will not
conflict with the values implicit in the formal authority
system.

A Basis for Estimating Management Development Results

Figure 1 shows in abbreviated form the basic conditions required to achieve each of the changes just discussed. The objectives of development efforts are listed across the top of the
table. Below each objective are the conditions that facilitate
achieving that change. For example, those conditions listed in
Column I will lead to increases in knowledge. The conditions
in Columns I and II will lead to attitude change. The conditions for development are grouped by rows according to participant characteristics, learning effort, leadership climate,
formal organizational goals, and organizational culture.

Developmental objectives can be attained without following
the above sequence exactly. For example, it is possible to
change managerial planning behavior by making a manager
responsible for preparing long-range planning documents and
capital expenditure forecasts. But if such a requirement is
not preceded by education and practice in the use and application of long-range plans, and if the manager is not given an
opportunity to discuss the desirability of such planning for
his own particular purposes, he will probably offer resistance
the first several times he is required to prepare a long-range
plan. Perhaps more importantly, the inefficiently prepared plans
may confuse more than enlighten his superiors, peers, and
subordinates. Nevertheless, a change in his budget or planning
performance is possible. For example, as a result of preparing several plans, the manager may realize the advantages,
change his attitude toward planning, seek an understanding
of the purposes and applications of planning, and, consequently,
increase his budget efficiency and effectiveness. It appears
however, that this is the hard way to accomplish such a behavior change because little or no attempt is made to insure
understanding and acceptance prior to performance change.

The degree to which the conditions in Figure 1 are present

Figure 1.
CONDITIONS REQUIRED TO INDUCE CHANGE THROUGH MANAGEMENT DEVELOPMENT

		Objectives of Development				
		I	II	III	IV	V
		Change in knowledge	Change in attitude	Change in ability	Change in job performance	Change in end-operational results
			(Conditions in Cols. I + II)	(Cols. I & II + III)	(Cols. I, II, & III + IV)	(Cols. I, II, III, & IV + V)
Conditions for Development	Participant characteristics	Sufficient IQ — Sufficient motivation	Flexible attitudes on part of participants — Agreement with spirit of the material to be learned	Non-conflicting habits or personality traits		
	Learning effort	Direct method of instruction (programmed learning, lectures, films, reading, and so on) — Competent instruction	Discussion of on-the-job applications and personal benefits	Practice of desired abilities — Corrective training (therapy) to correct undesirable habits and behavioral patterns	Opportunity for on-the-job practice of newly acquired abilities	
	Leadership climate		Neutral or positive attitude of superior toward development	Superior's attitude and example consistent with desired change	Coaching, counseling, and periodic performance review by superior consistent with desired performance	Performance appraisal by the superior based on practices taught in the learning phase
	Organizational climate		Goals, top-management philosophy, and policies consistent with learning phase		Philosophy, practices, and precedents of the policy-making executives consistent with desired manager performance	Top management active support and interest in development — Incentive system designed to reward practices taught in the learning phase
	Organizational culture		Cultural conditions and social beliefs consistent with desired attitudes		Informal group rules and standards consistent with desired change	Positive employee and informal group attitudes toward desired change

indicates the probable degree of change that will result from a developmental effort. Although such estimates will not be precise, previous evaluations[15] have shown that where the conditions specified in the table have been present, there have been significant increases in knowledge, attitudes, ability, and job behavior.

Specification of the minimum required conditions is not possible at the present stage of research and theoretical development. Moreover, fewer conditions than those listed may actually be necessary to attain any of the changes in the developmental process. For example, a change in knowledge can occur despite the lack of a competent instructor, if a participant reads widely in a particular field and is able to interpret the readings for himself.

Summary

The two major purposes of this chapter were to introduce to the reader the concept of development and to explain why many attempts at improving managerial performance through planned learning programs have not produced measurable change. The major conclusion which we draw from our review of the social science research is that, to be effective, development plans must take into account the many factors present in the manager's environment. Not only must such environmental factors be considered during the planning stage, but when they are found to be barriers to development, it is necessary to treat them either before developmental efforts begin or as part of the developmental effort.

The following chapter will suggest concepts of development which are designed to account for and treat the factors in the organizational environment which previous research reveals to be important to the success of development efforts.

---

[15] See Appendix 1 for a technical review of these studies.

CHAPTER 2

ORGANIZATION AND MANPOWER PLANNING*

by Henry L. Tosi, Jr., and R. C. Dunnock

Management development is concerned not only with current managerial performance but also with planning for the future: having the right number of qualified men available to fill higher-level positions in five, ten, or twenty years. This long-range planning involves two major steps: 1) organization planning, and 2) management manpower planning. The planner must estimate what changes will occur in the organization during the designated time period and how many managers with what skills will be needed to staff the organization of the future.

Organization Planning

Organization planning is basic to successful development programs. Unless future needs are assessed, programs may be initiated at the whim of executives and in response to training fads. Following is a brief description of the various stages in organization planning:

Determine long-range objectives. The organization's objectives must be based on a projection of desired consumer requirements. This projection should include some analysis of general socio-economic and political trends, foreign and domestic competition, technological development, and changes in consumer behavior.

Quantify the objectives. For planning purposes, the long-range objectives must be quantitatively expressed. One appropriate method is to make a sales forecast in constant dollar

*This chapter and the following draw heavily from an article by H. L. Tosi, Jr., and R. J. House, "Continuing Management Development Beyond the Classroom," *Business Horizons*, Vol. 9, No. 2 (Summer 1966), 91-101.

amounts. Where possible, the forecast should be broken down by product line, including consideration of estimated new product development, expansion, decentralization, or merger. A more comprehensive discussion of forecasting techniques ⁻has been discussed in detail elsewhere.[1]

Estimate effects of technological change. Technological change continually modifies production and distribution processes. Machinery now performs many routine tasks previously done by men, eliminating the need for much labor and supervision. Improved duplicating machines, for example, have increased the productivity of clerical workers. Other tasks are being combined into single jobs, requiring workers with higher levels of skill and intelligence. Computers are making some repetitive decisions once requiring the time and attention of men. For example, as a consequence of increased use of information theory and computers, Leavitt and Whisler[2] predicted that the organization structure of a firm may look like a football sitting on a church bell; middle management would be materially diminished because of the increased programming of its decision areas. More recently, Whisler has revised his belief that information technology would routinize middle management jobs.[3] He now predicts that the most significant effect of advanced technology on middle management will be the creation of a man-machine system, rather than his originally projected all-machine system.

Research concerned with production and information technology will have a profound effect on the nature of the work performed by managers and operative employees. Although the impact of future technological change cannot be predicted precisely, forecasting the approximate parameters of planned technical changes and estimating the impact of such changes on the performance requirements of future managers is an essential step in organization planning and management development.

---

[1] See, for example, R. D. Crisp, *Marketing Research* (New York: McGraw-Hill Book Company, Inc., 1957).

[2] H. J. Leavitt and T. L. Whisler, "Management in the 1980's," *Harvard Business Review*, Vol. 36, No. 6 (November-December 1958), 41-48.

[3] T. L. Whisler, "The Manager and the Computer," *The Journal of Accountancy*, Vol. 119, No. 1 (January 1965), 27-32.

Determine number of operative personnel. This begins with an analysis of past sales in terms of the number of personnel required to produce them. By projecting the figure obtained, and by making adjustments for fundamental technological changes in the nature of present operations (e.g., changes due to mergers, acquisitions, changeovers to automated equipment, or changes in market territories or product line), a rough estimate of the future employment force can be developed.

This projected number of employees may be broken down into major organization divisions, or functions. For instance, the present distribution of workers active in the functions of production, marketing, personnel, and finance will provide some basis for determining sub-unit sizes in the future.

Determine staff assistance required. As the organization grows and as products change, different requirements will be placed on the staff organization. Increased hierarchical complexity requires more staff assistance for coordination and communication. Increased specialization of processes requires greater separation of the planning and executing phases of work. This, in turn, leads to hiring more staff planners. For example, as consumer tastes become more complex, an increased variety of skills will be required in the market research area. Also, in the manufacturing area, emphasis on technical skills in the operation of automatic equipment may increase the ratio of staff to line personnel. The personnel function will change with changes in the composition of the employment force, with a different set of procurement and training problems resulting from changes in the social and cultural environment, as well as with the different qualities and abilities required for performance.

Estimate number of managers required. Accomplishment of the above steps makes it possible to determine approximately how many first-line supervisory personnel will be required to manage the work force. Projection of the span of control (or number of immediate subordinates) of first-line supervisors by functional breakdown will yield some approximation of how many future managers will be required. When the number of first-line supervisors has been estimated, the organization planner can make some inferences about the number of managers required at higher levels.

There is evidence from small group research, individual psychology and management studies suggesting some strong support for the traditional concept that the optimum number of supervisors per manager is between five and nine. For example, Berelson and Steiner, in reviewing small group research, state that the number of people that can apparently be taken into account at any one time, as individuals, is between five and seven. They write that "formality in leadership emerges rapidly beyond that number, and so do subgroups."[4]

Several factors will affect the span of control. The organization planner cannot accurately predict the extent of the effect of each of these factors. However, as plans develop and more specific information becomes available, they should receive increasing consideration and attention. The following list, while not comprehensive, consists of some of the more important of these factors:

1) *Rapidly changing situations.* The greater the degree of emergency involved, or the greater the speed with which a situation changes, the fewer the subordinates that can be managed.

2) *Repetitiveness of work.* As the work becomes more routine, the number of subordinates can be increased.

3) *Contact required between manager and subordinates.* If the job requires much interaction with subordinates, then the span must be reduced or the executive relieved of other duties.

4) *Quality and availability of staff assistance.* The proper use of staff relieves the executive of routine and technical tasks. This frees time for supervisory contact with subordinates. The availability and use of staff executives should increase the span of control.

5) *Interaction and interrelationship of subordinates' work.* The more the work of subordinates in a given unit is interrelated and requires coordination by a supervisor, the smaller the supervisory unit should be.

6) *Competence of subordinates.* Where the subordinate

---

[4] B. Berelson and G. A. Steiner, *Human Behavior: An Inventory of Scientific Findings* (New York: Harcourt, Brace & World, 1964), 358-359.

members are competent and aware of organizational policies and requirements, the necessity for face-to-face supervision diminishes and the possible span of control increases.

7) *Competence of the manager.* Some managers are more capable of supervising larger groups than others. Specific capabilities, of course, must be determined in a relatively late phase of the overall plan.

Forecast tentative organization structure. On the basis of projections developed, as outlined above, it is possible to arrive at a tentative organization structure for the planning period. By analyzing the required number of personnel in each functional area, such as manufacturing, distribution, and finance, and considering the spans of control, it is possible to describe a tentative primary line organization and to estimate the organizational levels and the number of managers required. It may then be possible to generally define the major responsibilities of each position.

Obviously, the planned long-range organizational structure will be subject to changes as it is approached in time. Conditions will change after initial plans have been made. These will require alterations to the original plan. Additionally, there must be provisions for moving the current structure toward the planned. Both these problems may be approached with the use of "phase plans." "Phase plans" allow for revision of earlier plans, changes in economic conditions, or loss of key personnel. They are intermediate plans, implemented between the original plan and the time in the future a plan is to be fully implemented. The long-range plan may be broken down into "phases" with respect to time and organizational units. For example, at a known time in the future, a company may be planning a split-off or a merger. An event of this nature may provide for convenient implementation of certain parts of the long-range plan. The "phases" may be timed to coincide with major additions, planned changes in plant and equipment, introduction of new products, and retirement of key personnel. The form of organization at a given point in time will no doubt be different from the "ideal" structure originally conceived in earlier planning for that time.

Organization Planning: Summary

Thus far, we have only dealt with the determination of the number of people required to staff an organization at some point in the future. We must also be concerned and perhaps more importantly, with some approach to specifying the skills required. We now turn our attention to the determination of management needs and the skills which must be considered in selection.

Management Manpower Planning

Management manpower planning involves 1) using the organizational plan to determine how many managers will be needed and what skills they should have, and 2) deciding how to fill the positions that will exist.

Need Determination

Basic future requirements may be deduced from the long-range organization plan. Comparison of these requirements with an inventory of present managerial capabilities in the organization will identify future needs for additional manpower. These needs will exist because of: 1) retirement or resignation, 2) changes in existing positions and responsibilities, and 3) the creation of new positions.

Replacement Needs

By comparing the work staff that will be available in the future with positional requirements at given times, the number of additional personnel needed can be determined. Vacancies occurring through normal personnel attrition must, of course, be considered. Retirement dates and planned promotions or transfers may be obtained from existing records. While separations and deaths cannot be individually predicted, historical turnover ratios and actuarial data provide a basis for estimating future loss rates.

Maintenance of a personnel inventory will facilitate the determination of replacement needs. It should contain information regarding the qualifications of present personnel, as well as the degree to which they may be moved into key spots in emergencies. Because a complete backup of every executive would be costly, it may sometimes be desirable to develop managers with enough flexibility to fill several organizational positions.

Future Performance Requirements

Many of the requirements for future performance can be inferred from the long-range organization plan. For example, the plan may indicate that future decision-making techniques will require increased use of operations research and information technology. Subsequently, mathematical skills may then be used either as one of the criteria for initial selection or to become the basis of developmental efforts. The company can then begin or plan to begin training programs designed to equip employees to meet future skill needs.

Mann's conceptual framework offers some aid in making skill determinations for specific positions.[5] On the basis of a number of field studies of several levels in organizations, he has classified the skills required for effective management as 1) technical, 2) human relations, and 3) administrative.

Technical skill is the specialized knowledge and expertise a manager must possess concerning the functions of the departments for which he is responsible. Technical skill usually concerns a specific product, process, or analytic knowledge. For example, the technical skills of a manager of a marketing department would be those related to market research, market planning, and implementation of marketing strategies. *Human relations or interpersonal skill* concerns the ability to maintain a cooperative, satisfied work group and to motivate and assist subordinates through recognizing good work, coaching and counseling, and considering their needs and problems. *Administrative skill* consists of the ability to make decisions and conceptualize relationships directed toward achieving organizational goals. Administrative skill also consists of the ability to plan, set objectives, schedule, organize, delegate, and control the work of an organization.

Mann suggests that different organizational levels require different skills. At the lower supervisory levels, technical and

---

[5] F. C. Mann, "Toward an Understanding of the Leadership Role in Formal Organization," in R. Dubin, et al. (eds.), *Leadership and Productivity: Some Facts of Industrial Life* (San Francisco: Chandler Publishing Co., 1965), 68-103.

human relations skills are most important. At the higher levels, however, administrative skills assume major importance.[6] He also proposes that the skill mix varies for different stages of organizational growth and development:

> Early in the life of the organization, technical and human relations skills are probably more essential.... As the organization becomes more complex, administrative skills become more crucial. During periods of rapid change...upper level supervisory personnel have to draw more heavily on their technical skills.[7]

It seems, therefore, that while precise skill definition is neither practical nor possible, personnel and organization planners can use these three skill classifications as a basis for designing development efforts.

Requirements for New Positions

The projected long-range organization structure will yield an approximation of the total number of positions that will exist in the future. New position requirements may therefore be determined by projecting which present positions will be continued, which will be changed, and what new positions will be added. The use of phase plans permits changes in the overall plan, which may be necessary because of changes during the time between initial planning stage and project completion.

Meeting Estimated Demands for Managerial Skills

Selection and placement programs are the methods that organizations use to maintain a stream of personnel in organizational positions. Selection, in this context, may mean either selecting those who have skills they will need in the future or selecting people expected to respond to development. Hopefully, the new manager has skills that will be needed in the future or is thought capable of developing them, but he must also be capable of meeting some current demands of the organization.

---

[6] *Ibid.*
[7] *Ibid.*

A Suggested Selection and Placement Program

Bennett[8] suggests a two-stage approach to the selection and promotion of managers. This approach integrates selection and development.

During the initial selection phase, personal biographical and background data, interviews, and psychological tests are used to determine whether further investigation of a particular candidate is desirable. This investigation is an attempt to determine whether the individual possesses characteristics *which the company* believes to be correlates of job success and improvement through development.

Previous studies have suggested that motivation to develop and attitude flexibility are important requirements for subsequent development. However, current psychological tests proposing to measure these characteristics are not generally considered as accurate as, for example, measures of intelligence. Since most management development does not include highly complex or abstract subject matter, and since most managers have been found to be above average in intelligence (as measured by IQ), lack of learning ability is not generally a problem in development. Learning ability becomes a major consideration only when the development plan of the organization requires rapid learning or when the subject matter is highly complex.

Those who successfully pass this screening may be given classroom training, supervised on-the-job training, or some combination of both. Their first organizational assignment should provide superiors with an opportunity to make meaningful estimates of the individual's potential. When, and if, the candidate successfully completes this first phase, he enters the supervisory management ranks at the lower levels of the organization. After working in a supervisory position, demonstrating actual leadership skills, and successfully making the decisions required to carry out managerial responsibilities, he then becomes eligible for the second phase of the selection process which is used to fill higher level management posi-

---

[8] W. E. Bennett, *Manager Selection, Education and Training* (New York: McGraw-Hill Book Company, Inc., 1959).

tions. By this time, much more relevant performance data is available. Performance in first-level supervisory assignments provides better criteria for selection and tests managerial potential more accurately than pre-selection tests.

Summary

This chapter has illustrated a general approach that is required in order to effectively carry out development efforts. Very few organizations making substantial investments in development programs subject these expenditures to the planning, analysis, and consideration that would be given a comparable expenditure for equipment. We have suggested that development be based on better planning.

Estimating future organizational needs will result in several benefits. The personnel selection program may be based on the future requirements of the firm when the general skill requirements of future executives have been determined. Promotion decisions will be improved, since individuals can be channeled into positions which will allow them to practice skills which will benefit both themselves and the organization in the future. When deficiencies are noted in future skill requirements, the objectives of training efforts become obvious. For those engaged in the planning of developmental efforts, organization planning provides a basis for determining development activities and costs. Perhaps the greatest value of organization planning is the knowledge gained about the existing structure and members of the organization.

In the next chapter we will discuss the relationship of organization and manpower planning to establishing objectives for development programs, concluding with a suggested approach to designing and implementing programs intended to achieve development objectives.

CHAPTER 3

POLICIES AND MANAGEMENT PRACTICES SPECIFICALLY RELATED TO MANAGEMENT DEVELOPMENT

by Henry L. Tosi, Jr., and Robert J. House

In too many cases, management training has failed to produce measurable results. Frequently when managers who have been given sensitivity training return to their jobs, they are not any more considerate of their employees than when they left. Managers who have learned the use of financial tools often find they are unable to use them on the job because their superiors wish to retain existing procedures.

A good deal of theory and research advanced in the last several years suggests that management development efforts must be more broadly based and more than mere classroom exercises by being designed to fit into or change the existing organizational climate. Management development efforts will result in desired changes only when the executive leadership in a firm is willing to *support formal development with necessary organizational motivators and reinforcers.*

These motivators and reinforcers may take the form of top management decisions, policies and practices that motivate, guide, and reward the transfer of training from the learning situation to the job. The policies and practices which have the most impact as motivators and reinforcers for development are those concerned with the coaching, appraisal and compensation of managers. This chapter will specify those particular factors of the formal organization that are pertinent to management development and that are *within the control of top management.* Top management's consideration of these factors can aid in the design of policies and practices consistent with

31

the development needs of the firm. These factors have been developed in detail in the general business literature, but they have not, in general, been related to change.

There are five areas in which management policies and practices most directly affect the results of management development activities. Two of the five, organization planning and management manpower planning, were discussed in Chapter 2. The remaining three are performance appraisal, compensation, and line staff responsibilities. The force of these factors in shaping the day-to-day behavior of managers makes it imperative that they be consistent with, and complementary to, training and development efforts. This will build developmental objectives into the daily job of managing.

Peformance Appraisal

A properly used appraisal system acts as both a developmental technique and a strong reinforcing agent for desired behavior. As a developmental technique, the participant learns how his behavior has deviated from the development goals. The appraisal system becomes a reinforcing agent when criteria of appraisal are derived from the content of development programs.

We propose the use of dual criteria appraisals for managers going through development. Each manager should be appraised separately for 1) performance in his current job, and 2) achievement of developmental objectives. He should receive separate and appropriate feedback in each area.

Dual Criteria Appraisal Systems

On the basis of research on General Electric's experiences with performance appraisal, Meyer, Kay, and French point out that it is "unrealistic to expect a single . . . program to achieve every conceivable need."[1] In too many cases, managers are exhorted to use appraisal systems for diverse purposes such as changing subordinate behavior, determining compensation

---

[1] H. H. Meyer, E. Kay, and J.R.P. French, Jr., "Split Roles in Performance Appraisals," *Harvard Business Review*, Vol. 43, No. 1 (January-February 1965), 127.

increases, and making promotion decisions. The multi-purpose use of performance appraisal systems is perhaps one reason for their general ineffectiveness. Since it is difficult to develop criteria that are related to all possible appraisal objectives, they must be clearly formulated prior to the development of an appraisal system. Clear formulation of objectives will often make it more apparent that a single system cannot effectively reach both present and future goals. The result may be a system in which separate appraisals are conducted for performance in a manager's current job and for achievement of developmental goals. Although these two appraisals may be conducted independently, the criteria applied in each should be complementary.

Establishing Criteria for the Two Appraisals

Assuming that appraisal criteria are the basis for rewards such as promotion and increase in pay, they must reflect organizational objectives in order to induce employees to engage in desirable behavior. By relating criteria to job performance it is possible to reduce appraiser bias that ordinarily results from the supervisor's personal orientation toward the employee. McGregor[2] and Kelly[3] have severely criticized the use of personality traits as the basis for appraisal, pointing out that this type of performance appraisal may result in an employee devoting his time to achieving a good personal relationship with his superior rather than to doing his job. They further state that unless the criteria are directly related to the job, there is a strong possibility that the appraisal will be based largely on the personal relationship between superior and subordinate. A study by Kellejian, Brown, and Wechsler[4] supports this argument. They conclude:

---

[2] D. McGregor, "An Uneasy Look at Performance Appraisal," *Harvard Business Review*, Vol. 35, No. 3 (May-June 1957), 89-94.

[3] P. R. Kelly, "Reappraisal of Appraisals," *Harvard Business Review*, Vol. 36, No. 3 (May-June 1958), 59-68.

[4] V. J. Kellejian, P. Brown, and I. Wechsler, "The Impact of Interpersonal Relations on Ratings of Performance," *Public Personnel Review*, Vol. 14, No. 4 (October 1953), 166-170.

The personality characteristics of the superior which influence his ratings consist of those attitudes and personal needs that determine the way he sees himself and responds to the world around him. The components of the relationship between superior and subordinate which affect the superior's ratings are, for example, tensions, likes, and dislikes. Among the situational variables which influence performance ratings are the actual performance itself, the nature of the rating task, and the organizational setting.[5]

Dual-Level Criteria Applied

We propose the use of a dual-level appraisal system, aimed separately at current performance and personal development objectives. *First-level criteria* are those which would be used for evaluation of current performance. These standards are derived from the activities required to meet position requirements. These criteria would not be unlike a position description, which specifies activities for any incumbent in that position.

The second level of criteria should be used to evaluate those managers who have participated in development efforts. These will be much more individually oriented, depending largely on the nature of the program in which the manager was involved. Evaluation using these second-level criteria, as an adjunct to the basic appraisal system, will reinforce the development program content. The usefulness of *second-level criteria* will depend primarily on the successful development of first-level criteria. The following approach, combining management by objectives and the critical incident method, is suggested for the development of second-level criteria. First, the management development staff should state the specific objectives of the training process.[6] These should be specific behaviors which should become part of the manager's behavior pattern as a result of participation in development. Participants themselves, as a training assignment, might develop a list of incidents they think could be applied on the job. These could

---

[5] *Ibid.*, 170.

[6] The identification of valid training objectives and the role of top management in formulating them is discussed in Chapter 4.

then be discussed with the superior of each trainee. The superior and the trainee can then determine which of the particular incidents apply to present, and perhaps future, organizational assignments. They mutually set performance and learning goals which become appraisal criteria for determining the application on the job of specific policies, practices, and behavior that is part of the training content. In summary, the evaluation criteria at the second level are 1) derived from learning content, 2) individually oriented, and 3) based on job needs.

Problems with Dual-Level Appraisals

A problem that must be considered in this context is the difference of opinion among superiors in different organizational units in specifying critical incidents for evaluation criteria. Where a program includes participants from several departments, it is possible that one supervisor will be more lenient than others in the selection of incidents and goals. There are two possible approaches to solving this problem:

1) A reporting system could be developed whereby each training participant's second-level criteria incidents are centrally maintained. Review by the management development staff will determine if there is leniency or rigidity in the appraisal system, and advice or training can be used to encourage consistency.

2) A more effective solution would be to insure that superiors are capable of goal-setting and incident-determination by training them adequately in these areas prior to assigning them appraisal authority.

The Appraisal System and Peformance Review

Since the purpose of appraisal is to improve performance, the appraisee must be made aware of the need and opportunity for development. This requirement, however, poses an important problem. When the need for performance improvement is communicated to an individual, it frequently has a threatening effect that hampers performance improvement.[7]

---

[7] Meyer, Kay, and French, *op. cit.*, 123-129.

Thus we are faced with a dilemma. How can subordinates be provided with information concerning their own development needs and yet not feel so threatened that the information becomes useless?

A series of recent studies conducted by the Behavioral Research Service staff of General Electric Company, in cooperation with the Institute for Social Research at the University of Michigan,[8] suggests a solution to this dilemma. These studies indicate that chances for improved performance are significantly greater when performance appraisals are conducted by managers who have been considerate and supportive in their relations with subordinates, emphasizing the need to solve work problems and accomplish specific work improvement goals and de-emphasizing personal criticism and blame. However, when the appraiser is punitive, or when he seeks to place blame on the appraisee, performance review sessions result in significantly less improvement.

Thus, the resolution to the dilemma appears to depend not upon whether performance information should be communicated to appraisees, but rather upon the manner in which the information is conveyed. A supportive, problem-centered, improvement-oriented approach has a better chance of stimulating improvement than does a punitive, personally-oriented, blame-centered approach.

Timing Feedback

For performance review to have the desired effect on behavior, it should be given as soon as possible after an action, subject to evaluation, occurs. While it may be impossible to provide immediate feedback after each action, some consideration must be given to establishing an appraisal system which provides for something more than yearly or semi-yearly review. While the desired frequency is difficult to state precisely, findings from two studies suggest some guidelines:

1) Flanagan and Burns found that the number of appraisal

---

[8] For review of these studies see J.R.P. French, Jr., E. Kay, and H. H. Meyer, "Participation and the Appraisal System," *Human Relations*, Vol. 19, No. 1 (February 1966), 3-20.

incidents recorded by appraisers varies inversely with the time between appraisals;[9]

2) Meyer, Kay, and French found that employees more readily accept suggestions given in less concentrated form from that of comprehensive annual appraisals.[10]

The timing of feedback, then, has an impact on both the effectiveness of the rater and the subordinate's response to the appraisal. It seems that the most effective feedback method is frequent communication between superior and subordinate relative to the subordinate's performance. It is more readily accepted by the subordinate, and the superior is able to focus on more pertinent items.

Rewards and the Appraisal System

First-level criteria should be the primary, if not the sole, basis for salary administration. Meeting second-level criteria can be rewarded with financial or non-financial bonuses. In this way, managers performing equally well on the same job will receive the same basic pay even though one of them is participating in a development program. The size of the bonus awarded for meeting second-level criteria should reflect the desirability of the improvement, the degree of goal achievement, and the difficulty of the goal achievement. (The use of bonuses will be discussed in more detail later in this chapter.)

Compensation

Compensation policies also motivate and reinforce developmental efforts. Those should be related to established standards of performance, current and planned organizational needs, and the individual's successful attainment of job and development objectives. They should rest on an analysis of the objectives of the organization. Compensation policies must also be consistent with goals and desired practices that are intended to result from development, since the compensation system is intended to elicit individual behavior directed toward organizational goals. It will have both motivational and reinforcing effects on the behavior of the members.

[9] J. C. Flanagan and R. K. Burns, "The Employee Performance Record: A New Appraisal and Development Tool," *Harvard Business Review*, Vol. 33, No. 5 (September-October 1955), 95-102, especially 97.

[10] Meyer, Kay, and French, *op. cit.*, 127.

Because increased salaries are an important value for many managers, they will attempt to achieve performance goals that they believe will lead to higher pay. We do not mean to imply here that financial motivation is the only effective means of changing and improving behavior. Yet adequate compensation, either present or anticipated, is necessary *before* the services of any manager can be obtained. Therefore, the motivational aspects of compensation can hardly be ignored.

Compensation may also reinforce existing behavior. Over a period of organizational life, an individual learns certain behavior that is "acceptable." When he associates compensation with certain specific actions he has been performing, the compensation serves as a reinforcement of those actions. Therefore, whether the behavior is or is not desirable in terms of organizational effectiveness, compensation associated with that behavior by the individual will serve to *maintain and strengthen behavioral patterns.*

Compensation Related to Development

If compensation is to adequately reinforce development efforts, the following requirements must be met:

Consistency between development and compensation. There must be consistency between the behavior suggested in development programs and the behavior for which individuals are compensated. Insuring that this compatibility exists is an absolute minimum requirement. Anything less will be detrimental to development efforts. Members must not be rewarded when they engage in undesirable practices and should perceive potential rewards for accomplishing development objectives.

Reward for individual development-related improvements. If development improves a manager's performance, he should be rewarded with higher compensation. Basic increases should be based on evaluation against first-level criteria and used to determine a manager's performance in his present job. Salary ranges at each organizational echelon should be wide enough to allow for differential payment based on the individual's performance level. Some additional method of compensation should be considered for those who perform well against second-level criteria (those criteria derived from development objectives and content). If financial incentives can be related to this evaluation, the effect on behavior should be favorable. One method may be the use of a one-time bonus for those who achieve specific second-level objectives. Bonuses have long been used to increase performance levels of manufacturing employees and salesmen. However, the effectiveness of a bonus wears off if it becomes regularly expected.

Summary

Compensation should not be relied upon as the only incentive for development, since many others may be as effective in changing behavior. However, the continuing reinforcing effect of compensation has a long-run effect on individual behavior patterns. The development of managerial talent requires an equitable mode of compensation that guides and rewards the individual's contribution to the firm as well as his own personal development. Obviously, the compensation program must be integrated with the appraisal system. Long-run behavior changes will be largely a function of the degree to which the system of formal structural factors and leadership reinforcement is compatible with the desired behavior.

Line-Staff Responsibilities

What Staff Can't Do

Staff organizations can provide substantial assistance to line management in identifying development needs and methods to satisfy these needs. However, the establishment and maintenance of a challenging and stimulating climate for development must ultimately rest on the shoulders of line management.

Miles Mace, in his report of a one-year field study sponsored by the Harvard Business School, concluded that the "creation of a satisfactory climate (for development) depends upon factors of much deeper significance than open doors or amenities of social exchange."[11] Mace found that in those companies where developmental projects seemed to be most effective, top management maintained an active interest and participation

---

[11] M. L. Mace, *The Growth and Development of Executives* (Boston: Division of Research, Graduate School of Business Administration, Harvard University, 1950), 133.

in a vigorous ongoing developmental program. Where top management engaged in its own developmental programs, conferred with equivalents in other companies, required annual or semi-annual reviews of progress and personnel (coupled with frank and realistic discussions), maintained personal interest in subordinates, and consistently held a conscious "coaching attitude," greater satisfaction was reported by those persons interviewed in the survey.

Three Critical Aspects of Coaching

The three critical aspects of coaching as an integral part of development are 1) personal knowledge of subordinates' strengths and weaknesses and the assignment of tasks which develop skills and reduce weaknesses; 2) creation of an atmosphere of trust and truthfulness in which an employee may feel free to discuss his progress; and 3) the acceptance of the executive role as a supportive coach, as well as a director and controller. To be effective, this climate must include the physical, intellectual, and psychological availability of the executive to his subordinates. Because the executive is in a position of daily interaction with the subordinate, he has major control over the atmosphere for development. In effect, every executive is his own personnel officer. Personnel departments may be adept at augmenting training and development programs, but "affirmative coaching is a line, and not a staff, responsibility."[12]

Problems to Be Confronted

Based on informal interviews with employees at a wide variety of levels from among many companies, Mace concluded that the efficient and effective programs were characterized by an adequate resolution of the following difficult problems and situations:

1) Overt commitment to development accompanied by covert resistance to change;

2) The fear of middle management that development of subordinates endangers its position;

3) A "do-it-yourself" attitude of many strong, self-made

---

[12] *Ibid.*, 109.

men who call for similar talent beneath them but who cannot delegate authority which would enable talented subordinates to learn by doing;

4) Resistance to making a shift from a judgmental, task-oriented outlook to an active coaching frame of reference;

5) Fear of social and emotional contact with subordinates, thereby preventing counseling and appraisal from becoming integral parts of daily interaction;

6) Resistance to periodic progress evaluations and personnel appraisal;

7) Maintaining a "continuing developmental" frame of reference. (One-shot efforts seldom accomplish long-term goals of improved managerial skills);

8) Dealing with the realistic development potential of a given employee, creatively using his present talents as an alternative to dismissal. A corollary to this aspect is the need to identify the persons most capable of benefiting from development efforts and to design appropriate techniques for specific persons.

Defining Staff Limits

It is obvious from Mace's findings and the evidence from survey research on performance review practices[13] that the burden for success of management development efforts rests heavily on the line manager, especially the immediate superiors of the managers who participate in development programs.

This helps us define the limit for effective use of staff assistance in the execution of development efforts. Staff specialists, by virtue of their detached position and specialized training, are in a position to help line managers define the development needs of their subordinates. They can do this by conducting interviews with appraisers of subordinate managers, by analyzing position performance requirements, and by comparing the performance of managers with these requirements. They can assist the line managers by suggesting alternative approaches for the development of specific attitudes or skills.

[13] H. H. Meyer and W. B. Walker, "A Study of Factors Relating to the Effectiveness of a Performance Appraisal Program," *Personnel Psychology,* Vol. 14, No. 3 (Autumn 1961), 291-298.

The staff specialist in management development should be charged with the responsibility to 1) know about seminars, university programs, and specialized management courses that are available to managers of his organization; 2) be familiar with the various methods of management training and know when each of these methods can be effectively applied; 3) determine whether his organization has a need for a learning program designed and conducted for its particular needs and be able to either develop such a program himself or arrange for a competent consultant or specialist to design and present such a program; and 4) conduct frequent evaluations of the development efforts conducted within his organization and recommend improvements as the need becomes apparent.

Still, the establishment and maintenance of a climate conducive to the transfer of training to job situations remains the primary responsibility of the line organization. As Mace's findings suggest, the day-to-day climate for development depends primarily on the attitude and behavior of the line managers. Specifically, coaching, counseling, delegation, appraisal, and the allocation of rewards and punishments must be performed within the line organization.

Summary

We have attempted in this chapter to present some of the factors that may be mobilized by the management of a firm to bring about successful change as a result of development. The policies of the organization must be consistent with the changes desired from development efforts. Development efforts must be more than just a series of lectures or cases presented in a classroom situation. Organization structure and practices must supply the necessary motivation and reinforcement in order that participants are supported to change. The various decisions and policy areas discussed here can help significantly.

Too many firms make apparent commitments to development efforts without an awareness of possible consequences. They send executives "off to school" for development training and expect a change, or improvement, to occur. If top management is not willing to make policy decisions and commitments in the areas discussed, preferring instead to go through the motions of development by participation in college and intra-company programs, then they must recognize that improved performance is highly unlikely. Development then takes the same form as extra-curricular activities. Such activities may, of course, be highly satisfying to the participants, but such satisfaction might be more economically obtained by using different techniques.

If, however, improved performance through management development programs is what is being sought, then top management must consider alternatives to "extra-curricular approaches." The following chapter, for example, will consider a "commitment approach" to management development.

CHAPTER 4

DESIGNING THE ORGANIZATIONWIDE
DEVELOPMENT PROGRAM —
THE COMMITMENT APPROACH*

by Robert J. House

Early in our review of social science and business research concerned with management development (Chapter 1), it became apparent that many managers designing management development programs frequently make certain fallacious assumptions both about those participating in a development effort and about the environment in which the participants work. For example, most managers developing programs too readily assume that 1) the program participants have the necessary capabilities for development; 2) the program content meets the needs of the organization and its managers; and 3) the top managers and the immediate superiors of the participants will support the development efforts. What is needed is an approach which does not unthinkingly make such assumptions. Such an approach must ascertain the validity of these assumptions before the development program is designed and provide for corrective action in circumstances where such assumptions are found invalid.

We shall call the approach recommended here *the commitment approach* to management development. This approach is designed to change both the behavior of individuals and the organizational unit in which they work. It 1) is based on organizational and participant needs; 2) provides for teaching methods which suit the attitudes and learning capabilities of the participants; and 3) either changes or fits within the prevailing organizational climate.

*Adapted from the *California Management Review* Vol. VII, No. 3 Spring 1965, Copyright 1965 by The Regents of the University of California.

Figure 2
A COMMITMENT APPROACH TO MANAGEMENT DEVELOPMENT

TOP MANAGEMENT

Step 1: Top management determines developmental needs and objectives using the recommendations of the staff analyst.	Step 2: The staff analyst analyzes existing environment and determines readiness for change.	Step 3: Top management participates in feedback of climate analysis.	Step 4: To commits it mental ob responsib

MIDDLE MANAGEMENT

Step 8: Middle management learns and practices with help of supervisors.	Step 9: M commits i application after disc supervisor modificati here.)

LOWER MANAGEMENT

The process at this and lower levels is the same as that outlined for middle management.

Top management assesses entire program.

nt
op-

Step 5: Top management
participates in the design
of program content by
a. Formulating company
   philosophy of manage-
   ment, and
b. Stating philosophy in
   form of teachable principles and policies.
(This is part of the learning
process for management.)

Step 6: Top management
implements new policies
at own level after coach-
ing by the staff analyst or
consultant.

Step 7: Top management
appraises subordinates
against newly established
policies and conducts
developmental coaching and
performance review meetings.

ment

Step 10: Middle management
implements policies with
help of top management.

Step 11: Middle management
appraises and informs
subordinates as to adher-
ence to policies.

This chapter describes the commitment approach. The specific steps recommended here must, of course, be modified to meet the requirements of an individual firm. However, we believe the requirements for effective development will be met if the essential features described in each step are provided in the design of any organizational development effort.

Figure 2 illustrates the commitment approach in flow chart form. From this illustration it can be seen that the approach consists of a process of analysis, learning, commitment, and implementation. This process starts at the top of the organization and is repeated at each managerial level.

Step 1: Establishing Development Objectives

Some students of management have said, "If you don't know where you're going, any road will get you there!" Hence, the importance of step one. The following must be considered if aimlessness is to be avoided in establishing development objectives for any change:

1) State objectives in specific measurable terms.
2) Gear objectives to organizational needs.
3) Coordinate objectives with overall organizational plans.
4) Insure objectives do not conflict with expectations of organizational members.

Stating Objectives in Operational Terms

Since development is concerned with change, desired changes, to be operational, must be stated in terms which are sufficiently specific to suggest the particular operations necessary for accomplishment and to allow measurement of that accomplishment. An objective stated in operational terms might be, for example: "As manager, you are to prepare a yearly budget for your department." A budget clearly suggests specific operations if it is to be met, while its adequacy is also readily measurable at the end of a given fiscal period.

Gearing Objectives to Organizational Needs

The qualitative aspects of the development objectives should be established so that the desired changes in managerial skills and efficiency reflect the organization's actual needs and current problems. Many development programs have failed because the objectives established were merely mirror images of development objectives commonly used in industry. For example, it will be useless to train an industrial supervisor in general principles of discipline if what he really needs to know is how to apply the specific rules of his company.

A logical first step is to take an inventory of current problems. This inventory can be based on an interview sampling of opinions of all levels of management and employees.

Once the major and most pressing problems of the organization have been identified, it will be easier to determine how a development program can contribute to their solutions. Where the problems stem from lack of knowledge or understanding, a development program can make a substantial contribution. However, when the problems stem from poor communication from top management, incompetence in selected key positions, or inadequate technical factors such as budget and control systems, other approaches may be required. Under such circumstances, methods such as managerial replacement, reassignment of responsibilities, increased use of controls, and/or closer supervision might be used. Most frequently, the effective solution of major problems will require some combination of several of these approaches. Using development as an exclusive means for solving major problems and bringing about change will be effective only when the key members of the organization are already receptive to change. After the major problems are recognized, the method of their solution must be devised to supply those relevant organizational factors which are missing.

Coordination of Development Objectives with Overall Organizational Plans

The development program must be designed to assist the organization in meeting its long-range plans and goals. For development efforts to be geared to plans and goals, the strengths, weaknesses, and development needs of participating managers must be assessed, and the abilities of present managers to attain long-range objectives estimated.

Trouble frequently results because many programs are established without consideration of these factors. For example, it is unrealistic to teach the benefits of participative, decentralized management in an organization which is already headed by an authoritarian executive who insists on centralized controls and who has no intention of changing.

Two planning areas in particular should be reviewed during the formulation of the development objectives:

1) The relevant external factors concerned with future market conditions: sociological, economic, and technological trends affecting the organization. This requires a careful review of such factors as:

   (a) The organization's current and expected position within the industry; (b) general industrial, economic, and socio-business trends; (c) current and expected product and labor market requirements; (d) current government regulations and regulatory trends; and (e) expected technological change that may be relevant to the organization's economic progress.

2) The organization's immediate and long-range plans. A careful review of the following factors is required:

   (a) the specific managerial behavioral patterns required to meet the organization's long-range plans; (b) the projected cash outlay involved in meeting the development objectives; (c) the cost in organizational efficiency of commiting key executive time to the development of the objectives and the subsequent program; (d) the potential problem areas that may arise as a result of the organization's transition from its current operations and practices to the revised methods necessary to meet future external requirements; and (e) the present trends that may change the existing environment within the foreseeable future.

Having identified the major problems of the organization and the requirements which are anticipated in the future, we can compare the strengths and weaknesses of present managers with these requirements and estimate their ability to meet the long-range objectives of the organization. The result of this analysis should provide an organization with realistic plans for meeting its internal requirements in relation to its current and expected market position. This does not mean that even rationally established objectives can be easily met. It does, however, provide for solving or circumventing major problems that may be detrimental to the organization's progress in the development of required managerial talent.

Compatibility of Change with Expectations

In addition to meeting definite needs determined by considering plans and goals, development objectives must also be in accord with (or at least not oppose) the personal goals of the participants. Conflict between program goals and participant goals creates barriers, particularly slower motivation to learn and resistance to change.

Development objectives which deal with an individual's performance must also be compatible with his supervisor's expectations. When the boss expects behavior which differs from what has been learned in a development effort, serious problems may arise. The manager who sends his subordinates to "get developed" may, in fact, be their chief deterrent to job improvement.

Form for Stating Objectives

A precise statement of the development objectives, although a technical consideration,[1] is crucial to the design of the entire development program. When objectives are specified in advance, the necessary conditions can be spelled out, specific reinforcements ascertained, and methods of instruction determined. Specific objectives should be stated in the following areas:

Knowledge. The knowledge objectives, if stated precisely, describe the responses which the participant should make in reply to requests for information taught in the program. Paper and pencil tests can be used to measure knowledge achievement.

Attitudes. Objectives concerned with attitudes state the beliefs, convictions, and emotional responses which are expected of the participants as a result of the development. Question-

---

[1] For an excellent discussion of the requirements and methods of establishing developmental objectives, see Robert F. Mager, *Preparing Objectives for Programmed Instruction* (San Francisco: The Fearon Publishers, 1962).

naires, interviews, and direct observation can be used to measure attitude change.

Skills. Objectives concerned with the achievement of skills describe the actual behavior which the participants can exhibit under learning conditions. Skill objectives fall into two broad categories—intellectual skills and social skills. Skill achievement can be measured by the use of classroom assignments which simulate actual working conditions. Examples of such assignments are role playing, in-basket techniques, management games, and case problems.

Job performance. Objectives concerned with job performance state the desired responses to actual job situations and problems. Performance change can be measured through direct observation by the participant's associates, superiors, and subordinates.

End operational results. Finally, objectives concerning results specify desired changes in productivity, cost, scrap, employee turnover, group cohesiveness, grievance frequency, and the like. The first four objectives, when achieved, serve as intervening variables to bring about improved operational results. Operational results are stated as organizational output rather than individual performance. When records are maintained by areas of managerial responsibility, and when responsibilities are clearly defined and separated, operational results can be measured by the use of managerial performance standards.

For example, suppose that the general topic of a development program for plant managers is long-range facilities and manpower planning. Objectives for this topic concern knowledge, attitudes, skills, job performance, and end operational results and are illustrated below:

Knowledge: The participant should be able to answer such questions as: "What are the basic considerations and steps involved in developing a long-range plan?"

Attitudes: Given a questionnaire on planning, the participant will agree with a statement such as, "A superior can often anticipate and either eliminate or minimize emerging problems by devoting a fixed

portion of time to long-range planning on a month-
ly (or quarterly) basis."

Skills: In a case situation, the supervisor will be able to
to use economic, financial, and manpower data
to develop a long-range plan to meet the requirements of the case.

Job performance: One month after training, employees of each
supervisor who participated in the course will
indicate on a questionnaire that they and their
supervisor initiated work on the development of
long-range plans for their unit.

End operational result: Key positions will be filled without
the use of temporary "acting" incumbents. Production costs and scrap rates decrease with improvements in production facilities.

Once these objectives are specified in the form mentioned
above, the sequence of learning activities and the actual conditions which permit, or give rise to, the desired responses can
be determined through analysis. Provisions can then be made
from the beginning for necessary learning activities, required
environmental conditions, and the measurement of program
accomplishment.

Step 2: Analysis of Existing Climate

After determining the objectives of the development effort,
the existing environment must be considered in order to identify
major deviations from ideal conditions. Conditions are ideal
for the development of managers when the circumstances
listed below are present.

Ideal Conditions for Development of Managers

1) Managers at all levels in the organization understand
   the overall objectives of the business.
2) The basic principles, intentions, values, assumptions and
   beliefs of top management and each manager's superior
   are communicated and understood.
3) The particular functions or activities of each member of
   the organization are clearly understood by that member
   and by those with whom he deals.

4) Responsibility and authority have been delegated to the extent that each manager is challenged by his responsibilities and has the opportunity to make decisions and mistakes and to profit from these mistakes through guidance from his superiors.

5) Control and accountability have been established so that each manager has adequate information and guidance for periodical review of both his own and his subordinates' performance.

6) Current managerial practices do not conflict with the intent or prescriptions of the management development program.

7) Managers are willing to make the necessary commitment to change, to coach their subordinates, and to learn new skills themselves.

8) The informal organization and the personal beliefs and attitudes of non-managerial employees do not conflict with the objectives of the development effort.

9) Top management has the confidence of the members of the organization, and it is viewed as a good place to be employed.

10) The members of the organization are not experiencing anxieties resulting from such factors as punitive leadership practices, role conflict, role ambiguity, or excessive job pressures.

The degree to which actual conditions vary from the above determines the degree of need for environmental change as a part of the development effort.

Analyzing an Organization's Environment

Several factors need reviewing in order to obtain an adequate assessment of the organization's environment. Such an assessment should indicate the degree to which the above basic conditions are present by including a careful analysis of the following factors:

1) *The published policy structure.* A review of policy structure should include analysis of current published policy and procedures, past changes in basic policy guides, and changes

that are planned. Inconsistency among present policies or inconsistency in policy decisions over time indicates a problem either of poor communication or of inadequately formulated management philosophy. If the published policy structure is practiced, it is a good indication of the organization's basic management philosophy.

2) *Current established management practices.* Many practices that are not formally authorized become a routine part of the organization and soon carry the weight of policy. A trained observer can usually identify such practices through discussion with members at all levels of the organization; while the staff, as a result of working closely with top management and having access across functional lines to all levels of line management practices within the organization, is usually more aware than are the line employees of these unauthorized routine practices.

3) *Formal delegated authority within the organization.* Inconsistency in delegation practices suggests lack of attention to organization design. This deficiency may result from a lack of awareness of the importance of consistent organizational practices. For example, an organization lacking a formal compensation program may indicate authority through informal procedures and signature approval lists which authorize key decisions and expenditures as well as the organization's functional grouping and relative salaries for each position.

4) *Informal authority within the organization.* Informal authority (or influence) becomes evident when discussion with members of the organization results in constant reference to particular individuals who review major decisions prior to implementation, even though the decision in question may be outside the individual's area of formal responsibility. Those persons whose influence is evident, but is not reflected in the form of formal delegation, are very important in determining the organization's philosophy.

5) *Formal organization structure.* Formal organization structure consists of charts published by the organization for internal use. Past as well as current organization structures should be reviewed to determine trends or basic changes in operating philosophy and practices. Recent basic changes in reporting

relationships and functional groupings may indicate trends or major changes in management practices.

6) *Available measurements.* The social sciences have developed and made available a number of methods for analyzing environmental conditions. Massel[2] has validated a scale designed to measure the degree to which policy is understood, practiced, and perceived throughout an organization. Allen[3] describes methods of responsibility and authority analysis for determining the consistencies of gaps and overlaps in delegation practices within an organization. Likert[4] discusses survey methods which can be used to assess human relationships pertinent to management improvement. General Electric[5] has developed a check list of questions designed to help a manager analyze the climate in which he works and to determine development needs. And, while structured interview, observation, and analysis of the content of administrative documents are other useful approaches to the analysis of developmental conditions, it should be noted that research and methodological development are far from complete. Obviously, the use of the above methods is best handled in conjunction with a well-trained and skilled management analyst.

Step 3: Feedback to Top Management

The third step is a report of the findings to those with the authority to change existing conditions when deviations from the ideal are discovered. Such a report brings beneficial information, critical to the success of a program, to top managers who become actively involved in development. Experience indicates that this feedback results in lively and operationally-centered

---

[2] M. Z. Massel, "An Audit Method with an Application to Management Programs for Determining Differences of Opinion Within and Between Policy Makers, Policy Implementers, and Policy Receivers," unpublished Ph.D. dissertation (Evanston, Ill.: Northwestern University, 1958).

[3] L. A. Allen, *Management and Organization* (New York: McGraw-Hill, 1958), 162-164.

[4] R. Likert, "Measuring Organizational Performance," *Harvard Business Review*, Vol. 36, No. 2 (March-April 1958), 41-50.

[5] General Electric Company, *Manager Development Guide Book I: Managerial Climate of the Organizational Component* (New York, 1956).

discussions concerning the causes of variations from the ideal environment.[6]

Several benefits result from well-designed meetings. First, top management (which has the necessary authority to use information effectively) becomes actively involved in development because information critical to the success of the management development program is brought to its attention. Second, the meetings provide an information flow between management levels and an impetus for continued definition and clarification of policy and top managerial objectives. Such communication usually becomes necessary for a complete implementation of change. The ability of an organization to accept, understand, and use self-criticism through pre-designed communication channels is, of course, invaluable.

Obviously, newly established communications channels are applicable to more than a formal approach to development. Dependent upon an organization's initial environment and problems, this critical feedback may well be one of the primary values received from the implementation of a formal development program. On the basis of top management's analysis of the existing organizational climate, the staff analyst can list the environmental factors which are most likely to inhibit effective development. These factors must be eliminated, while the development needs resulting from current problems and long-range plans must be achieved either prior to, or as a result of, the development program. Thus, the original statement of development needs and objectives enlarges at this point to include a statement of environmental factors which inhibit effective development.

Assuming that the staff analyst is highly competent in identifying managerial problems and in researching pertinent literature, he can now be guided by the list of development objectives, current problems, and inhibiting environmental factors in determining how available research, theoretical literature, and experiences of other organizations apply to the problems of his particular organization. This description of

---

[6] For a case study which reports the results of such a feedback meeting, see R. J. House and J. M. McIntyre, "Management Theory in Practice," *Advanced Management*, Vol. 26, No. 10 (October 1961), 16-22.

the analyst's tasks assumes that he is not only thoroughly familiar with business and behavioral science literature, but also is soundly trained in conducting management audits.

On the basis of his survey and determinations, the analyst then suggests various alternatives aimed toward effective development. For example, one such alternative might be to change current planning practices. Another might be to define managerial responsibilities more clearly. Top management enters into discussion of the merits of these alternatives and suggests other possible alternatives. The analyst's job here is to point out the development implications of the various alternatives, as evidenced by previous research, experience, and theory. Top management's job is to point out implications of the local situation which may require unique treatment. Thus, the analyst acts as theorist and top management as expert practitioner. If the analyst is familiar with the previous research and theory pertinent to the problems of the organization, his efforts, combined with top management's knowledge of the particular requirements, and peculiarities of the organization, should result in an optimum mix of the benefits of theory, previous research, and experience. In the many cases in which findings based on earlier research or experience of other organizations are applicable, top management will be able to decide immediately to install new methods or practices to meet the needs of their particular management team. In other cases it will probably be necessary to conduct one or more staff studies to determine policies, methods, and practices which meet the requirements of the particular organization.

Often an analyst must indicate where management has failed to provide an adequate development climate. If top managers refuse to accept the findings in light of the evidence presented, or if they are defensive about their own practices, then the variations between the existing and the ideal environment are a measure of the degree to which development will be hampered.

Step 4: Management Commitment to
Development Responsibility and Objectives

If top managers are receptive to the findings resulting from the analysis of their existing climate, and if they exhibit a willingness to consider suggestions for improvement and change in existing climate where necessary, development can begin. But, the development process will not actually begin until top management makes commitments and assumes responsibility for improving those organizational practices found to conflict with development. Expressed willingness for change should be obtained from the managers at the policy-making levels. These key managers should be informed of the improvements that change can effect and, at the same time, forewarned about problems that often occur and require solution throughout the entire change process. In particular, it is important to insure a clear understanding that not only do these problems frequently arise, but also that their solutions may require commitment to new management practices rather than to tradition or precedent created by past solutions to similar problems. Commitment based on an understanding of the costs and benefits of the development effort provides a foundation for total organizational development and begins the process of climate-conditioning at the top prior to development effort at the lower levels.

Management commitment is probably the most critical requirement for the success of any development effort. For, if development efforts do not consider changing the development environment when necessary, and if such efforts do not take place *through decisions* by top management, an overall change in performance *cannot* be expected or predicted. Research indicates that under such conditions the best that might be hoped for is a change in the managerial performance of a few of the individuals in the program. However, individual changes usually are not sufficient to improve overall organizational performance.

Possible Conflicts Resulting from Development

A program which conflicts with existing objectives, policies, tradition, and management practices, or with the informal organization, and which is conducted without top management participation, is not only unlikely to succeed, but it is also very likely to result in serious, undesirable effects such as anxiety, disappointment, bitterness, frustration, and uncertainty. These result primarily from 1) being personally threatened by the changes introduced; or 2) being thwarted in attempts to apply advanced concepts learned to the job situation. For example, if a participant perceives the course content as sound and applicable to his job but encounters resistance when he applies it in his work environment, his effectiveness may actually *decrease* as a result of his disappointment and uncertainty.

In short, if a development effort is to succeed, top management must meet these two fundamental requirements: 1) active participation in the establishment of the development program, and 2) acceptance of responsibility for providing an environment conducive to development.

Step 5: Top Management Participation in Program Design

The role of top management in program design is to participate in the selection of program objectives and to participate in the learning process necessary to achieve these objectives. Top management's evaluation of program content is based upon readings and survey results provided by the staff analyst, as well as upon its own experience with the organization.

Once top management expresses a willingness to consider management development topics, the staff analyst can review existing documents, policy manuals, and administrative directives to assess the degree to which formal practices are compatible with the process of development; he can now also interview members of top management, sampling managers at every level in the organization, to analyze climate and development needs. Such interviews not only seek recommendations for topics to be discussed by top management, but also try to identify problems confronting the members of the organization. In short, the staff analyst offers a list of suggested topics based on his research and seeks top management consideration.

In reviewing the results of the needs analysis, top management now modifies or approves the topic list on the basis of both its knowledge of the environmental factors and the analyst's list of problem areas as viewed by subordinate levels of management. Following modification and/or approval of the topic list, the analyst provides reading assignments designed to inform the top managers of the basic considerations which enter in the development of policy (or set of policies) for each topic discussed. Texts or current periodicals serve as primary sources for these reading assignments. For example, if the topic to be discussed is "management communications," the analyst selects readings in the general area of communications. These readings might cover such subjects as information flow, semantics, employee and management information needs, the nature of the grapevine, and managerial communication responsibilities.

Members of top management, after reading the assignments for a particular topic, meet to discuss the policy considerations involved. If the managers find they already practice the recommendations in the readings, they then document the practices in the form of policy. Such documentation should consist of a statement of the basic principles, assumptions, intentions, beliefs, and convictions of top management concerning the particular topic, together with action guides to carry out the principles. If, as a result of the reading and discussion, management decided that the amount of available information has not been sufficient to make a policy decision, it might authorize additional study to resolve questions. On the topic of "management communications" mentioned above, such an authorized study might include a review of attitude surveys, studies in information and control theory, and studies concerning the information needs of the employees and managers in that organization.

Even with these bases for decision making, it is not certain that managers will choose the best program content. Ideally, managerial practices and styles of managerial behavior and leadership should not be taught until they have been proven applicable to the particular organization. However, extensive testing and evaluation may be prohibitively time-consuming and expensive. If behavioral science research does not suggest solutions that have worked in similar situations in the past, and if top management lacks the practical background for dealing with existing conditions, it may be advisable to conduct research within the firm to determine which of the alternative solutions produces the desired results.

Having agreed on program content, top management must

go through the prescribed learning process and/or adopt the newly established policies to provide an example for their subordinates.

Advantages of the Commitment Approach

The advantages of designing the program in this manner are that the content finally approved by management is 1) an expression of the policy and philosophy of the firm; 2) realistic in terms of applicability to the organization; 3) based on a top management commitment to the course content; and 4) understood and practiced by the top managers of the firm.

Step 6: Decision Implementation

Development requires that policy decisions be implemented at each successive level of management concurrently with, or immediately prior to, instruction on how to carry out those policies. Requiring top and middle managers to apply new policies brings out difficulties in practice that the development program does not cover. Changes can then be made before subordinate managers are given incomplete or confusing information in the development program. This method provides higher level managers with the advantage of "learning by doing" and provides subordinate managers with knowledge not only of the fact that new policies are being practiced, but also of how they are working.

Since the list of decision topics may cover as many as thirty policy areas, establishing program content may take as long as a year. Implementation of such decisions, even if begun immediately after the decision is made, may require an additional six months. This suggests that implementation of all policy decisions may delay the development program for the lower levels as much as two years. Such a long time is required because this approach attempts to change the environment as well as the individual manager. This is a long, delicate, and sometimes painful process. A large time gap is not always necessary, however, since a program can be started at the second level as soon as a sufficient number of policy decisions have been made *and implemented* at the top level. Initial policy commitments at the top level provide program content for the initial meetings at subsequent levels. Such decisions also demonstrate the active participation of top management to managers further down in the organization. Under optimum conditions, implementation of new policy decisions appears to take a minimum of six months.

Step 7: Supervised Job Practices

If the new knowledge and attitudes acquired in a formal training course are to be translated into improved abilities, practice is required to give the participant confidence in the ideas and techniques being taught and to eliminate the errors which usually accompany the practice of new skills.

The abilities which are developed will be utilized on the job *if* the supervisor insures their use through supervised practice, increased delegation, coaching, counseling, and appraisal. The essential requirements for on-the-job practice are: (1) the participant should understand how his performance compares with standards of desired performance, and (2) the participant should be rewarded or censured, depending on his performance.

The first of these requirements is met via a periodic, planned performance review in which the participant's performance is discussed with him so that he can correct any errors in his performance. The second requirement is usually met through the initiation of policy statements.

If reward or censure for specific actions is to improve performance, it must be administered by the participant's supervisor. To administer reward and censure from other points in the organization would require the participant to be the "servant of two masters," thus increasing the likelihood of role conflict.

In addition to the need for top management support and for supervised job practices, there is also the need to insure that the formal policies and practices of the organization will reinforce the objectives of the development program.

Summary

This chapter has recommended a particular approach to organizational improvement through management development. Development objectives are derived from policy decisions by top management. These decisions are based on readings, surveys of lower-level managers to determine what they think problems are, and top management's own specific knowledge of conditions within the organization. If any of these sources indicate that the organizational environment will interfere with development, these problems are treated before initiating the development process. These policies are adopted first by top management and then by progressively lower levels of management. This provides an example for groups that are to learn new procedures and insures that managers who use methods learned during development will not find that these conflict with those used by their superiors.

The training of each group involves not only reading, lectures, and discussion, but practice in new skills during training and on the job where each participant is guided by his immediate superior. The participant meets with the supervisor periodically to discuss his performance and to determine how he can meet standards if he has not done so. Thus the approach recommended combines the values of both a planned learning effort, with its motivating and reinforcing policies and practices, and a "learning by doing" type of experience which involves the immediate superior as well as the participant.

We now turn to look more closely at developmental methods, particularly at those which are commonly used in developing managerial personnel.

CHAPTER 5

DEVELOPMENT METHODS

by Henry L. Tosi, Jr.

Organizations have experimented with a great variety of techniques for instruction, coaching, and self-development, resulting in a wide range of development methods now in use. This chapter will focus on the more commonly used methods and will suggest how these induce different kinds of changes, or what have been called "objectives of development." (See Figure 1, Chapter 1). The following discussion begins by making a fundamental distinction between techniques used in on-the-job and off-the-job settings.[1]

Off-The-Job Methods

Training activities generally occur in some place other than the individual's job setting. Program content may be varied, and instruction periods may range from one day to several weeks or months. Most off-the-job methods provide a great deal of information to a large number of people at one time, thus reducing the "exposure-to-training" cost per person. As stressed in Chapters 2 and 3, this may be false economy unless some provision is made for transferring the learning back to the job.

Lecture. The lecture is probably the most widely used training method. In the lecture, an "expert" presents information verbally to the participants. Teaching aids such as flip charts, flannel boards, and films may be used to heighten interest and facilitate the teaching. The content of lectures may vary, of

---

[1] For a more detailed discussion of some of these techniques, see W. Wikstrom, *Developing Managerial Competence: Changing Concepts, Emerging Practices* (New York: National Industrial Conference Board, Inc., 1964).

course, from human relations to such technically complex subjects as operations research. The lecture is a vehicle for the presentation of information to a very large group of people at one time, which may be responsible for some of the lack of measurable results associated with development programs using lecture techniques.

Lectures are more effective for imparting conceptual knowledge rather than for changing attitudes or behavior. The learning situation is removed from the job, the learner is essentially passive, and most lectures are not supplemented with follow-up to insure transfer of the knowledge to the job. In summary, lectures can increase knowledge of the sort that is measurable by a paper and pencil test; usually, however, they affect job behavior little, if at all. They can have indirect effects on behavior, however, when used in conjunction with other training methods such as on-the-job coaching by supervisors.

Discussion techniques. Discussion methods involve the trainee more actively in the learning process. In *instructor-centered group discussion,* the instructor structures the learning situation for the group. He makes assignments, asks questions, and answers the participants' questions. This method consists primarily of instructor-student interaction sequences. The effectiveness of this technique in a particular situation depends largely upon participant preparation. Unless the trainees have some knowledge of the subject matter prior to meeting, the training session frequently resembles more a lecture than a discussion.

Student-centered group discussion techniques are similar. In contrast to instructor-centered group discussion, the major interaction patterns are student-student, rather than instructor-student. The primary role of the instructor is to serve as a moderator, keeping the group on the subject, stimulating discussion by asking probing questions, and acting as a resource when the group is otherwise unable to secure needed information.

One variant of the student-centered discussion technique is the *case method.* Here, participants are presented with facts in a decision situation (real or hypothetical). Each student separately analyzes the facts and works on his own solution to the case problem. In the classroom, the students examine and discuss their analyses and recommendations. The basic purpose of a case study is to create a learning environment which will involve the participant in decision-making processes and in developing methods for coping with similar problems in his "real" world.

Group decision-making is an extension of all types of student-centered discussions. Here each trainee goes beyond the learning processes involved in both instructor-centered and student-centered discussion methods by deciding for himself whether he will attempt to apply the content of his teaching to his job. The decision is a public or private commitment to implement the practices that are the subject of training.

When a participant has made a commitment to act in a particular way and is able to see his decision as compatible with an emerging attitudinal consensus of the group, his attitudes and behavior are more likely to change. A review of the literature also indicates that while the instructor-centered method is effective in changing knowledge levels, student-centered methods and group decision-making techniques are more likely to change attitudes and behavior.[2] For example, Levine and Butler compared the formal lecture method with group decision-making as alternative methods to induce 20 supervisors of 395 factory workers to overcome bias in performance ratings.[3] The results showed that only the supervisors involved in group decision-making improved their ratings, while those in the lecture group persisted in commiting rating errors.

Role playing. In role playing, the participants act out various parts in a situation related to problems which are the subject of training. The situations normally involve the interaction of several persons. Roles are assigned to various participants. For example, one trainee may act as a product manager and another as a customer complaining about the product. Each

2 R. J. House, "Managerial Reactions to Two Methods of Management Training," *Personnel Psychology*, Vol. 18, No. 3 (Autumn 1965), 311-319.

3. J. Levine and J. Butler, "Lecture versus Group Discussion in Changing Behavior," *Journal of Applied Psychology*, Vol. 36, No. 1 (February 1952), 29-33.

participant improvises his assigned role within guidelines set by the instructor. Other participants observe the players. When the process is completed, the participants and the observers review what took place and discuss its implications. Role playing may be used to illustrate sets of relationships between people in operational situations. Grievance handling, conducting appraisal interviews, and sales situations are appropriate subjects for role-playing sessions. Role playing may be especially useful in developing social skills such as coaching, counseling, and interviewing.

Some problems are attendant in role playing. Participants must be familiar with the role content before it is attempted. Unless foremen have some knowledge of the grievance procedure, using grievance-solving situations will benefit them little. Another problem is that participants may view role playing as more of a "game" then a learning experience and, therefore, they may not act as they would if faced with the given situation on the job. The trainer must be skilled in preparing the participants for role playing and in explaining its purpose and dynamics.

Role playing has succeeded in stimulating changes in both behavior and attitudes. In one study, Speroff combined a group therapy approach with role playing to increase supervisory understanding of the relationship between an individual's personality dynamics and on-the-job problems. After a six-month training program, the supervisors' personal effectiveness in handling grievances was nearly doubled over an eight-month period.[4]

T-Group training. The primary purposes of such training, according to the National Training Laboratory, are 1) to provide leadership with the sensitivities and skills necessary to more effectively guide and direct changes in social arrangements and relationships; 2) to develop in leadership an understanding of, a sensitivity to, and skill in participating effectively as both leaders and members of group processes; and 3) to

---

[4] B. J. Speroff, "Group Psychotherapy and Role Playing in Labor Relations: A Case Study," *Group Psychotherapy*, Vol. 14, No. 2 (June 1960), 87-93. The measure used was the rate of grievance disposition under conditions of heavy grievance load for the supervisor.

discover and develop tested principles and improved methods of human relations training. The Personality Institute of Industrial Relations at the University of California takes a rather broad approach in stating the objectives of sensitivity training as directed toward the development of both social sensitivity and behavior flexibility. This means that this training method seeks to produce both attitudinal and behavioral changes. These changes are not to be made in a specific direction pointed out by the trainer; instead, each trainee is encouraged to get a better look at himself and to experiment with new, perhaps personally more appropriate behavior.[5]

Sensitivity training is founded on the belief that human relations, understanding, and skillls can be developed through re-education, and that the aim of training is to make the participants feel, think, and thus behave differently about the human relations situations they are likely to face.[6]

T-Group training involves an attempt to replicate the "human side" of organization. Such training provides the participant with an opportunity to experiment, invent, devise, and test ideas and methods so that he may see how they affect himself before he employs them with others.

Participants are placed in small, unstructured groups. No goal is provided, and the trainer does not provide content structure as in other methods. The participants must then search for and develop behavior to facilitate group operations. They receive systematic feedback and analysis of the interaction processes which have occurred. When participants find that previous behavior patterns are not effective in resolving problems, they "search" for different, presumably more effective, patterns.

Argyris summarizes what he believes the laboratory method should provide the members of the group:[7]

---

[5] R. Tannenbaum, I. R. Wechsler, and F. Massarik, *Leadership and Organization: A Behavioral Science Approach* (New York: McGraw-Hill, 1961), 125.

[6] C. Argyris, *Interpersonal Competence and Organizational Effectiveness* (Homewood, Illinois: Dorsey Press, 1962), 134-137, 145.

[7] C. Argyris, "Yourself as Others See You," *Business Week* (March 16, 1963), 160-162.

1) An opportunity to expose their behavior as well as their thinking.
2) An opportunity to receive feedback.
3) Creation of an atmosphere where members are willing to expose values, attitudes, and feelings.
4) An opportunity to "intellectualize" the learning into a rational, consistent, cognitive framework.
5) An opportunity to experiment with new ideas, values, and behavior.

Recent T-Group controversy. At a Cornell University conference on management development in New York City, Odiorne severely criticized sensitivity training on the grounds that 1) it is not training since the objectives and process have not been well defined, are not well understood as yet, and are not within the control of the instructor; and 2) it has been known to result in serious mental disturbance for the participants. Odiorne reports having witnessed a serious mental breakdown precipitated by participation in a T-Group training program.[8]

In rebuttal, Argyris said that there have been only four nervous breakdowns among 10,000 participants and "all of these people had previous psychiatric histories."[9] He stated further that "a trainer can only go so far in preventing destructive experience." The important thing is that people "can decide how much they want to pay psychically" for what they are learning. Argyris maintains that T-Group training is *not* psychotherapy, though it does aim to change behavior. "Openness and trust are what we want to develop." However, Argyris agrees that the technique ought not to be conducted for lower supervisory levels, for as one member of the conference suggested, "Wouldn't this mean stripping a man of his defenses in the areas he needs them most?"

Other than those mental disturbances cited in the debate between Argyris and Odiorne at the Cornell conference, our survey of the literature revealed no documentation of mental disturbances resulting from T-Group or sensitivity training

---

[8] G. S. Odiorne, "What's Wrong With Sensitivity Training?" Paper presented at the Cornell Conference on Management Development, New York, (February 28, 1963).

[9] C. Argyris, "Yourself as Others See You," *op. cit.*

effort. However, such negative results are not likely to be reported widely in published form.

In addition, there has been argument over the ethical propriety of the T-Group method. Specifically, this argument centers on whether sending an employee to such training does not constitute an invasion of privacy. Proponents argue that the probing involved in the T-Group process concerns areas of the participant's life that are not directly related to the job and are not the concern of the company.

> They further argue that when an organization sponsors T-Group programs and participation in them is "suggested" by one's superior, attendance cannot be considered strictly voluntary. Therefore, T-Group training, when suggested by a superior, becomes an invasion of personal privacy.[10]

Recent studies have revealed that T-Group training is a powerful method for bringing about change in perceptions, attitude, and behavior. However, these studies also reveal that T-Group training may have an undesirable effect and that the outcome of the T-Group experience may be harmful to the participants.[11] At present, it is virtually impossible to predict the consequences of T-Group training for any individual or organization. The limited evidence concerning the conditions required for effective use of T-Groups prompts us to recommend that this be used only for experimental methods, conducted under conditions permitting careful observation of the emotional responses of particiants. We further recommend that such experimentation be conducted only by completely competent personnel, preferably with some clinical training.

Business games. A business game is an attempt to simulate a business environment by using mathematical models to represent economic variables such as supply, demand, firm and industry behavior, and costs. A game is usually played by several teams, each representing a firm competing for a given market. In the game, team members make decisions ostensibly

---

10 See R. J. House, "T-Group Education and Leadership Effectiveness: A Review of the Empiric Literature and a Critical Evaluation," *Personnel Psychology,* Vol. 20, No. 1 (Spring 1967), for a review of this controversy.

11 See *Ibid.* for a review of this research.

similar to those that might be encountered in actual business operations. The game may be extremely simple or very complex, and may be built around any and all functional areas of business.

Games are intended to illustrate the complexities and interactions of decisions in the real world; to show the importance of such concepts as long-range planning, organization, and specialization of function; and, to provide an environment in which technical skills, such as linear programming, may be used in a quasi-real situation. While there is no direct evidence suggesting the extent to which games accomplish these objectives or influence job behavior, they do provide players with an opportunity to examine, on a smaller scale, the complexities, interactions, and effects of decisions on operations. The game however, can be nothing more than an oversimplification of a real situation. Also, the game's designer builds his own biases into it. A good or bad decision, then, is what the inventor believes it to be. What is true in the game may be untrue in real situations. Therefore, in selecting a game, one should have a clear objective in mind and be certain the game unambiguously illustrates the points desired to be emphasized.

Summary

Thus far in our discussion we have suggested a legitimate place for off-the-job development techniques, finding them to be relatively effective in increasing knowledge by exposing new material to large numbers of managers at the same time, thus reducing the cost of training. Most importantly, however, these techniques can facilitate the application of improved methods by reducing resistance to change. If they are successful, the manager learns and develops favorable attitudes toward the content of training, which results in increased willingness to transfer training content to his job. Those who are concerned with the development process will have to provide an organizational system and climate compatible with the training objective in order that this knowledge and skill transfer can be facilitated. There is no question that it is only on the "firing line" that management potential can be fully developed. Reliance upon off-the-job methods alone, therefore, should not be expected to change job performance. Changed behavior results only when off-the-job methods are used *in conjunction with* on-the-job methods.

On-The-Job Methods

We now turn to a discussion of development activities and practices that have as their setting the manager's day-to-day work environment, considering as development only those efforts which have some explicit or implicit learning or improvement objective. Normal progression through an organization, even though learning occurs, does not fit the development concept unless there is some intended individual improvement rationale behind the moves.

Rotational programs. Job rotation, with its expressed purpose of improving managerial competence, has long been used as a development strategy. In rotation systems, the manager moves from job to job, usually at planned intervals. In most cases, the jobs vary in content and function. It is not uncommon for an executive to work for a period in sales, then production, then finance, and so on.

In horizontal rotation, job assignments are at the same organizational level. A trainee may act as foreman, first in a shipping department, then in a quality control department, and then on the production floor. A vertical rotation plan may be designed so that a trainee begins in advertising, then receives a promotion to a higher position in marketing research, and then a still higher position in sales management.

Rotation plans may be used to provide the trainee with a perspective of the organization. He may be exposed to the functions and activities required to operate different departments, obtain a first-hand consideration of the interdependencies of organizational components, and see the similarities and the differences in techniques required for effective management of work groups. However, for information, guidance, and development, the trainee must rely largely on the personnel within the department to which he is assigned. They may view him as a threat to their position or feel that he is only "passing through." In any event, they may devote less time than they ideally should to aiding his development.

There is no empirical evidence to date on the effectiveness or ineffectiveness of job rotation. Until investigation is carried out, job rotation should be assumed to be neither more, nor less, effective than other on-the-job training methods that do not include systematic coaching and use of feedback.

Understudy methods. Any method in which an individual is trained on the job by a single higher level executive falls into this category. This includes the positions of "assistant" and "assistant to." Understudy methods may also be combined with rotation plans; i.e., a trainee might work as an assistant for several executives during his training tenure.

Generally, the trainee learns the job assignment of his superior by observation, work on special projects, routine delegation of authority, and discussion. This method may be used to fill the impending vacancy of the superior or to equip the understudy or assistant with the knowledge and skills he will need when he is assigned a regular management position. While the understudy approach does provide the trainee with experience and knowledge about a particular job, ineffective management practices of the superior may be perpetuated.

Understudy training may be used after a man has been selected for a position, but before the incumbent has been moved, and be particularly valuable when organization stability is critical. The loss of key personnel should have less impact when individuals with knowledge of these particular jobs are available.

As with rotation, there is no empirical evidence supporting or rejecting this method. It should be viewed as another alternative method of providing a trainee with experience.

Special assignments and committees. Assigning managers to special projects or special committees has been used as a development method. Perhaps the most widely known technique is "multiple management" as used by McCormick and Company.[12] There, lower-level executives in various functional

---

[12] H. F. Merrill and E. Marting, eds., *Developing Executive Skills: New Patterns for Management Growth* (New York: American Management Association, 1958), 141-147; J. C. Baxter, "Multiple Management Motives: A Case History," *Personnel Journal*, Vol. 35, No. 7 (December 1956), 254-257; and D. W. Blend, "Point of Decision," *Dun's Review and Modern Industry*, Vol. 68, No. 1 (July 1956), 40-41, 94-97.

areas serve on "boards" to study problems and recommend solutions to top management. These are studied, reviewed, and considered for adoption. If they are not implemented, the reason for rejection is usually fed back to the proposing "board."

This method provides lower-level executives with first-hand experience in working on actual problems and attempting to solve them within the structure of the organization. Multiple management or committee assignments can be especially effective in developing the interpersonal skills of the manager, since he must deal with others in meetings of the "board." As with rotation and understudy methods, the effectiveness of committee assignment has not been thoroughly researched. There is no doubt, however, that they provide valuable experience and exposure to the trainee.

Performance appraisal. This method has been discussed in detail previously in Chapter 3 of this book. Performance appraisal provides the participant with feedback regarding his performance. An individual is required to demonstrate his managerial techniques or behavior on the job and is subsequently informed about the quality of his performance as measured by certain criteria, or standards of performance. When there is a difference between actual performance and the performance standards, the reasons for the deviation are identified through an appraisal interview and probing discussion. The supervisor then counsels the lower-level manager on how to improve his performance and provides him with additional practice and feedback.

Performance appraisal may be used as a development method or as a reinforcement for other methods. The dual-level technique suggested in Chapter 3 is appropriate in either case. If it is used as a development method, the superior and subordinate may simply agree on improvement objectives, which subsequently become second-level criteria left to the discretion of individual managers and possibly resulting in problems of inconsistency in development objectives throughout the organization. Solving such problems requires a conscious effort on the part of top management to formulate, communicate, and effectively implement a set of development objectives as guides for lower-level managers to use in developing improvement objectives for their subordinates.

On-the-Job Methods — A Comment

It is important to distinguish between the evaluative aspect and the development aspect of on-the-job methods. As development methods, these techniques imply much more than simply monitoring a manager's performance. They must be a vehicle through which a superior can provide his subordinate with feedback about his performance, give suggestions for changing his behavior, and, more importantly, *permit him to function* in a climate which allows him opportunity to experiment with different behaviors without fear of negative sanctions.

Considerations in the Selection of Method

A fundamental consideration in selecting teaching methods is that of management's attitude toward them. Generally, managers more readily accept methods such as lecture and programmed learning, which are primarily instructor-centered with little interaction among trainees (such as conference leadership methods conventionally practiced today), than trainee-centered methods involving a high degree of interaction.

Highly permissive methods of instruction, furthermore, tend to make managers impatient due to their questioning of the teacher's competence and of the importance of such training methods. A more structured method, however, significantly improves management's attitudes toward training. For example, House[13] found the use of leader-centered techniques useful in gaining acceptance of management training efforts. Prior to introduction of the leader-centered method in one company, the managers had frequently complained that trainee-centered discussion was inconclusive and non-applicable.[14] After introduction of more directive learning techniques, class attendance, course completion, and voluntary enrollments in manage-

---

[13] R. J. House, "An Experiment in the Use of Management Training Standards," *Journal of the Academy of Management,* Vol. 5, No. 1 (April 1962), 76-81.

[14] R. J. House, "Managerial Reactions to Two Methods of Management Training," *op. cit.*

ment training courses increased significantly. At the beginning of the experiment, it was difficult to induce managers to attend the management training classes. By the end of the experiment, however, seventy-five managers had asked to attend subsequent classes or had requested permission for their subordinates to attend. Under normal conditions managers are almost always task-oriented. Task-oriented groups, possessing high need for achievement with high demands on their time, quickly become impatient with activities which do not yield at least some results in short periods of time.

One might conclude from the available research that the desirable learning sequence for management development involves 1) a straightforward, leader-centered presentation, such as a lecture or selected readings; and 2) a discussion of the implications of the material as it relates to on-the-job practices of, and apparent benefits to, the participants. Participant discussion of the benefits and applicability of course content, therefore, takes up where leader-centered presentation leaves off in facilitating attitude changes. For example, House's study of managerial reactions to leader-centered and trainee-centered methods reveals that participants prefer leader-centered methods *when new material is introduced,* but, when once familiar with the subject matter, they prefer trainee-centered methods. Perhaps this is so because discussion allows the participant to: 1) reflect on the knowledge content of the program; 2) weigh the advantages and disadvantages of applying what he has learned; and 3) compare his thoughts with those of other participating managers and supervisors in the program.

Limits to Leader-Centered Training

Increased knowledge and changed attitudes readily brought about through leader-centered training methods are usually, in themselves, inadequate in changing behavioral patterns; also required is corrective effort such as feedback, together with supportive climate changes, the principles of which are reviewed as follows:

*In the feedback technique the participant is asked to demonstrate his managerial practices or behavior and is then informed as to how his behavior compares with the practices taught in the program.

*Where a difference exists between the participant's performance and desired behavior, the reasons for the deviation are identified through probing and discussion.

*Attempts are made to correct the deviation through subsequent practice and feedback.

Summary

In discussing general methods and techniques commonly used in developing managerial personnel, we have drawn upon the development objectives described in Chapter 1 and developed in Chapters 2, 3, and 4. We have distinguished between off-the-job and on-the-job development methods, noting both the appropriateness and limits of each approach. Usually, it is a combination of methods, beginning with leader-centered and moving toward trainee-centered, and a follow-up of off-the-job programs with on-the-job efforts that results in changing behavioral patterns of managers, and, indeed, the organization as a whole.

The following chapter examines means by which development programs may be evaluated and even predicted. "Was it worth it?" and "Will it be worth it?" are the questions to which we now turn.

CHAPTER 6

THE EVALUATION OF MANAGEMENT DEVELOPMENT

by John R. Rizzo

Introduction

Why evaluate?

Organizations that undertake a management development program have the right to ask, "What are the results?" "Was it worth it?" "What did we get from it all?" Yet there are strong indications that the right to question the effectiveness of development is seldom exercised. A variety of training is being conducted in organizations, but evaluation of it is frequently conspicuous by its absence or inadequate when present.[1]

Some organizations rightfully expect proof that their investment in development yielded some sort of payoff. In this case, evaluation is inescapable. Other organizations hold to the philosophy that development is intrinsically good, and in so doing, appear to justify their investment. Although the justification may satisfy them, they may fail to realize that development efforts and outcomes can often be substantially improved through the knowledge gained from a sound evaluation. Evaluation can take many forms, and can suggest answers to many questions.

It seems, then, that whatever the attitude toward development, evaluation is needed. This chapter attempts to provide guidelines for conducting evaluation of a development effort.

---

[1] W. McGehee and P. W. Thayer, *Training in Business and Industry* (New York: Joh nWiley & Sons, 1961), 277-284; and V. H. Vroom and N. R. F. Maier, "Industrial Social Psychology," *Annual Review of Psychology*, Vol. 12 (1961), 413-446.

What does evaluation involve?

This question can best be answered by first briefly examining some antecedents to a development program, as well as certain aspects of the development effort itself.

Typically the organization recognizes the need for development: problems may become apparent; planning could reveal gaps to be filled or goals to be attained; research or analyses might lay bare some glaring weaknesses; and so on. Whatever the source, a commitment to development is made. The organization may then set out to systematically determine specific aspects of its needs in relation to its goals. From this the program takes shape. Goals are defined; desired changes are specified; groups to be trained are identified. Training methods are selected. Plans regarding timing, coordination, and expenditure are made. Consideration is given to methods and criteria to be used in the evaluation of the development effort.

This, then, is the setting. It is basically a situation in which needs and goals are to be met through a systematic attempt to induce change. And, wherever possible, the desired changes are linked to defined organizational goals.

Evaluation of the development effort involves two major aspects. The first is the definition and measurement of *criteria* to be used in the investigation of whether or not change occurred. In order to demonstrate change, measurements must be taken. Development is a "before and after" situation, and as in the classical diet advertisement, we need a measure, or criterion, like weight, to show that change occurred. The diet in our case, of course, is the development effort.

The second aspect lies in the experimental design. Every effort should be made toward establishing and executing a good research design. The purpose of a good design is to demonstrate changes *and* to be able to reasonably attribute these changes to the development effort. Let us consider each of these two aspects of evaluation in more detail.

The Criteria

There are virtually hundreds of criteria which could be used as indices of changes as a result of management development.

The organization and its operations — and the personnel who are responsible for both — comprise a complex situation which can be viewed and measured from many vantage points. With this as a background, let us examine the criterion problem.

What Are Some Typical Criteria?

A few examples of criteria are listed below using an outline consisting of five "Objectives of Development." The list is not intended to be exhaustive. Furthermore, as we shall see later, it is possible to classify criteria under several headings. That is, criteria are not always independent; in fact, they are usually interrelated. And they may be used as indices of more than one organizational condition or goal.

Changes in knowledge
— of human relations principles and practices
— of management principles, methods, and theory
— of company goals and policies
— of technological advances

Changes in attitude
— toward the company; its practices, philosophy, policies, goals
— toward immediate supervision or top management
— toward co-workers
— toward subordinates, or *of* subordinates
— toward development efforts

Changes in ability
— human relations skills: communication, interpersonal skills, leadership ability
— work skills: communications, planning, coordination, control, budgeting, decision-making
— reduction of poor past habits

Changes in knowledge, attitude, and ability as a result of development must manifest themselves on the job and in the organization; criteria, therefore, also reflect:

Changes in job performance
of the participant
— actual management practices: the application of

human relations and work skills (above) to the job situation
— technological innovations
— number of profitable suggestions
— per cent of management who perform well
— turnover, absenteeism

of the participants' subordinates

— suggestions, innovations
— productivity, improved performance
— satisfaction and morale
— turnover, absenteeism, grievances
— scrap records, down time

Changes in end-operational results

This could include all of the above, as they are reflected in organizational
— policy changes
— technological advances
— personnel and production records
— cost reductions
— activity changes: more time spent in planning, coordinating
— structure changes: new staff services

It should be kept in mind that some criteria on this list suggest a single measurement (e.g., absenteeism), while others suggest a number of measurements (e.g., satisfaction: with pay, benefits, supervisory practices, etc.).

What Forms Can Criteria Take?

The forms that criteria can take may be described as follows:

(1) *Ratings* — judgments of ability, performance, products, or ratings of satisfaction with various factors.

(2) *Questionnaires* — of a variety of types to measure decision-making, the solutions to problems, attitudes, values, personality, and so on.

(3) *Tests* — written examinations or performance tests, for example, to tap changes in ability or knowledge.

(4) *Observational techniques* — to measure skills, ability, communication, productivity, and so on.

(5) *Company records* — either existing records or those devised for the evaluation of development; to measure production, turnover, grievances, suggestions, absenteeism, and the like.

It is immediately apparent that there are many available forms of criteria, for the above list may be expanded to include various types of questionnaire approaches, several types of performance tests, and so on. Each of the five general types suggest considerations too numerous to be elaborated upon. Before a development effort can rightfully take place, however, the form, content, length, specificity, and the administration of criterion measurement must be decided upon. Each form requires skill and knowledge in its construction, use, and interpretation.

What Are the Sources of Criteria?

It is a relatively simple matter to enumerate sources of criteria. Development programs take place in an organizational setting; it follows that in seeking sources to gather our data for the purpose of evaluating development, we can turn to:

(1) the participant in development
(2) the participants' immediate superiors
(3) the participants' more remote superiors (e.g., top management, directors)
(4) the participants' subordinates
(5) other non-participants in the company (for comparison purposes)
(6) company records
(7) persons outside the company who might be affected by the development program

Different sources may be selected to demonstrate a single idea: attitudes may be of interest regarding the participant or his subordinates. Or the same source may be approached to demonstrate several ideas; e.g., a participant may hopefully change with regard to both knowledge and attitudes.

Furthermore, information gathered may be grouped in several ways in order to make comparisons of different kinds: by function, by department, by organizational level, and so on.

The combinations are numerous. They should be given ample consideration prior to the development effort, keeping in mind the goals of the effort.

What Should Be Considered in Selecting Criteria?

In addition to form and source, there are a number of other criterion characteristics to consider. A knowledge of these is indispensable in selecting and developing good criteria.

Relevance. A good criterion must be relevant to the goals and intentions of development. Backtracking for a moment, it will be recalled that one of the antecedents to development involves the recognition of need. From this, development goals are established which should relate to the organization's goals. Unless the criteria used to evaluate development reflect these goals, and are relevant to them, they are to a great extent without meaning and hardly justifiable. Authors such as McGehee and Thayer[2] argue for organizational analyses, operational analyses, and man analyses in order to determine more adequately and specifically needs and goals. If this is done, criterion relevance is more easily attained and demonstrated.

Bias. Good criteria must be free from bias. Bias can occur in a number of situations. For example, supervisors (of development participants) who favor development may bias their performance ratings of participants in a favorable manner. This could occur consciously or unconsciously, perhaps as a result of searching harder for improvement in the participants' behavior.[3] Participants may bias a criterion such as an attitude questionnaire to give a favorable or "expected" impression, or even an unfavorable one, depending upon their feelings toward development or the organization. Bias can even occur in the selection of criteria, or in the interpretation of the results of a program. It is often difficult to prevent bias, but understanding the criterion and the conditions under which development takes place can help immeasurably in identifying and perhaps controlling it.

Reliability. Criteria should demonstrate consistency of meas-

---

[2] McGehee and Thayer, *op. cit.*, chapters 2, 3, and 4.

[3] H. C. Smith, *Psychology of Industrial Behavior*, 2nd Ed. (New York: McGraw-Hill, 1964), 307.

urement made at different points in time, all other factors being equal. For example, if a participant's score on a test is high one day and considerably lower or higher on the next with no apparent cause for the change, the test may be very unreliable. That is, it does not produce the same measure twice for an individual. If measurements fluctuate because of unreliability, it would be impossible to use these measurements to attribute changes to development efforts. Development may have had an impact, but it takes a reliable measure to demonstrate this.[4] Independent checks on the reliability of a criterion should be made where the reliability is unknown. When standardized printed tests or questionnaires are used, information about their reliability is often available.

Practicality. This takes on several meanings, with cost usually the underlying reason. Some observational techniques or performance tests may be unjustifiably expensive or time-consuming to administer and evaluate. Of course, this is a matter of judgment, and depends heavily on the goals of the program. Criteria may also be rendered impractical because of their relative unavailability. They may take too much time to develop or too many man hours to acquire. If plant conditions must be altered (or not permitted to change) in order to acquire a criterion (such as production records), there is a good chance that this would be highly impractical. It also may be experimentally impractical to have to wait too long after the end of a development program to measure a criterion; if too much time passes, factors other than the development program could affect the measurement.

Acceptability. Criteria must be acceptable, first of all, to the top management in the organization who make the final decisions regarding the development effort. They must see the importance and relevance of criteria before they can be used. Acceptability to the participants is important as well. They may be resistant to or offended by some criteria. Certain personality

4 For discussions of this complex problem, see: R. L. Thorndike, *Personnel Selection: Test and Measurement Techniques* (New York: John Wiley & Sons, 1949); J. P. Guilford, *Psychometric Methods*, 2nd Ed. (New York: McGraw-Hill, 1954); J. P. Guilford, *Fundamental Statistics in Psychology and Education*, 3rd Ed. (New York: McGraw-Hill, 1956); and E. F. Lindquist, ed., *Educational Measurement* (Washington, D.C.: American Council on Education, 1951).

tests, peer ratings, performance tests, or observational techniques, under certain conditions, might be highly objectionable to participants. Their use might conceivably create conditions which would be difficult to overcome. Hopefully, the acceptable criteria will be those which meet the other standards of good criteria.

Objectivity. An objective criterion is one which is more apparent and quantifiable and less subject to bias in interpretation. It is to be contrasted with a subjective or vague criterion which is easily subject to bias. Objectivity is a relative matter. Rating scales, for example, are more objective than anecdotal descriptions of performance. Measures of output may be more objective than ratings of productivity. It is often argued that objective measures are more readily available at lower organizational levels than at management levels (criteria such as production indices, scrap and breakage, accidents, etc.). In actuality, criterion problems exist at all organizational levels. Many factors operate to make apparently objective criteria poor criteria. Poorly kept work records, shift differences, machine or supply irregularities, and the like, can contaminate the so-called objective criterion. And these problems are more often the rule than the exception. Good objective criteria are available at all management levels; knowledge tests, attitude scales, measures taken on subordinates, and cost accounting measures serve as examples.[5] The question is more one of judicious selection, development, and measurement of criteria rather than it is a giving in to difficulties and a taking of "what comes along." In general, objective criteria should be sought and developed. And, if some subjective data is gathered (essays, letters, memos), provision should be made for the most objective evaluation possible.

Each of the foregoing aspects of criteria is important in its own right. Weakness in any one aspect is not easily overcome, and certainly not by strengths in another aspect. Relevant impractical criteria are as useless as practical irrelevant ones; un-

---

[5] H. E. Brogden and E. K. Taylor, "The Dollar Criterion — Applying the Cost Accounting Concept to Criterion Construction," *Personnel Psychology,* Vol. 3, No. 2 (Summer 1950), 133-154.

reliable acceptable measures are as useless as reliable yet unacceptable ones.

Each of the aspects of criteria should be used as standards to evaluate the selected measures, preferably in the planning stages of development. Management and other experts should be consulted to insure that these standards are met.

Criteria may also be described along another set of dimensions. They need not actually be evaluated along these dimensions in the sense of meeting certain standards, but such dimensions as the following should be considered in the planning stages of a development program:

(1) *The time factor*. Planning should include a decision about *when to measure* the criteria selected. Typically, measurements are taken prior to and following the development effort: the "before and after" paradigm suggested earlier points to this conclusion. However, measurement during training may be helpful in determining the intermediate impact of development—in order to better chart change (because it may be more appropriate) or even to help plan the course of development. Furthermore, measurements may be taken immediately after development as well as at several points in time afterward. The more time that elapses after the termination of training, however, the more caution needs to be exercised in attributing changes to the development effort.

(2) *Directness-indirectness*. Direct measures are those reflecting and taken from the participant himself (e.g., knowledge test scores). Indirect measures reflect changes measured through other sources such as subordinates (e.g., their satisfaction, productivity) or through the use of records (e.g., those reflecting absenteeism, grievances).

(3) *Specificity-generality*. An example of a specific criterion would be a score on a single attitude dimension (e.g., satisfaction with benefits). A general one might be an overall performance rating.

(4) *Multiple criteria*. Very often, a number of simple, specific criteria are amenable to combination into more global indices. These measures may be combined on the basis of expert

judgments. This could be done prior to the development effort, when it would be decided that certain specific scores (e.g., scores on individual attitude items) should be combined into an overall score (e.g., one which would indicate level of satisfaction or morale). Specific and combined scores would be interpreted in the analysis of results. This could easily be part of the predevelopment effort, especially if sufficient attention were given to criteria at that time. After development begins, and data become available, statistical approaches to combining measures may be used. Various correlational approaches in statistics are designed for this very purpose. A qualified statistician would be needed for this, and the approach would be helpful in understanding the empirical relationships and groupings of the measures.

How Should Criteria be Selected?

The selection of criteria depends on many factors, some of which have already become apparent.

The primary basis for the selection of criteria lies in the goals of the organization, since it is these that are reflected in the goals of the development program. If these goals are made explicit and established in planning the development program, an excellent effort toward meeting the standard of relevance is already under way.

The standards of bias, reliability, practicality, acceptability, and objectivity should likewise influence decisions regarding criterion selection.

The nature of the training method may dictate the form and content of the criteria. Complex performance tasks often yield subjective essay material to be analyzed.[6] The criteria must then be developed through objective analysis of the essay material, perhaps in the form of expert ratings. Group discussion techniques suggest criteria such as attitudinal and personality measures. They further suggest the possibility of

---

[6] This reference to a "complex performance task" can be best understood by referring to N. Frederiksen's following articles and book: "Factors in In-basket Performance," *Psychological Monographs,* Vol. 76, No. 22 (1962); *Factors in In-basket Performance* (Princeton, N.J.: Educational Testing Service, 1961); and, with D. R. Sanders and B. Wand, "The In-basket Test," *Psychological Monographs,* Vol. 71, No. 9 (1957), which describes the test itself.

observational techniques, ratings, and so forth, which could dictate the form and nature of the criteria. Technical training could lead to the use of criteria tied directly to the specific content of the training (e.g., speed in the execution of an assembly process).

The examples are virtually endless. The selection of criteria, then, depends upon the goals of development, whether they meet certain standards, and the nature of the training method.

The criterion problem is a complex one, and no argument can be too forceful that calls for constant attention to the selection and development of good criteria. As Smith states, "With no criterion, no evaluation is possible, and no progress can be made."[7]

The Criterion Measurement Problem

Written tests, performance tests, questionnaires, rating scales, reliability, objectivity, multiple criteria — all these and other terms so freely used are really starting points for a host of measurement problems. Some quick examples: there are many ways to design a test or questionnaire, there are many forms of rating scales, there are a number of ways to determine reliability, and there are several complex statistical methods to combine criteria. Furthermore, the evaluation of development requires a reasonable knowledge of experimental design, and of data analysis and interpretation.

Many texts are devoted to these topics.[8] The average manager would easily be overwhelmed by these problems. The obvious indication here is that a person well trained in test and scale construction, experimental design, and statistical analysis, should be consulted in the planning and execution of an adequate development evaluation. This is a necessity for under-

---

[7] Smith, *op. cit.*, 308.

[8] See, for example: A. Anastasi, *Psychological Testing* (New York: The Macmillan Company, 1954); L. J. Cronbach, *Essentials of Psychological Testing* (New York: Harper, 1949); E. E. Ghiselli and C. W. Brown, *Personnel and Industrial Psychology*, 2nd Ed. (New York: McGraw-Hill, 1955); Guilford, *op. cit.*; Lindquist, *op. cit.*; E. F. Lindquist, *Design and Analysis of Experiments in Psychology and Education* (Boston: Houghton-Mifflin, 1953); and B. J. Winer, *Statistical Principles in Experimental Design* (New York: McGraw-Hill, 1962).

standing and in planning the future course of many organizational activities suggested by development efforts and results.

The Experimental Design

Let us return once again to the "before and after" characterization of development. Because organizations are so complex, a number of factors can and do operate to produce changes. In this sense, the development program can be viewed as one, among most likely several, of these factors.

In the evaluation of development, the organization seeks, in addition to increased understanding, some evidence of the program's effect upon it. The existence of good criteria is one necessity in this quest, but it is not enough. Some sort of control must be exercised in order to demonstrate, with reasonable assurance, that the changes which occurred are attributable to the development effort.

Common-Sense Control

Given the aim of evaluating development effects, it is a matter of common sense to take steps to reduce, or at least account for, the effects of factors not associated with the program. For example, assume that a group of managers are participants in a human relations training program. Assume further that the criteria of interest are the number of subordinate grievances, and various measures of participant and subordinate satisfaction. Suppose that during the development effort, company policy changes are instituted that permit the participants to be more considerate of subordinates (e.g., more time is permitted to consult with subordinates, more freedom to grant rewards is allowed, etc.). These policy changes could obviously have an impact on the criteria cited, and so could the human relations training. It is impossible to say which is responsible.

This somewhat oversimplified example should caution management to be aware of even more subtle effects. Of course, an organization must make some changes apart from the development effort. It has a function to perform which cannot be postponed or subjugated to maintain control for the sake of evaluating development. To refrain from using a production innovation, in aiming for better evaluation, would be a costly step indeed, and most likely not worth it. An awareness of extraneous effects, however, is required in obtaining development evaluations.

Many of the headaches of evaluation can, to a great extent, be overcome through the use of control groups, a discussion of which follows.

What Are Experimental and Control Groups?

Those who undergo training, the participants in the program, are identified as the experimental group. Another group, similar to the experimental group but which does not participate in the program, is identified as the control group.[9]

The principle underlying the use of these groups is simple. It may be stated as follows: if the groups are similar and face similar experiences before, during, and after development *except for the exposure to a development program,* then changes which occur in the experimental group and not in the control group can more reasonably be attributed to the development program.

What Can Be Said When Control Groups Are Not Used?

Suppose criterion measurements are made only *after* development without the use of a control group. Smith states the situation aptly:

> Taking measurements after training is the easiest method of evaluation...students attend a course ...(and)...take a test...From their test scores, what can be realistically concluded about the effectiveness of the training? The answer is: almost nothing. While the test scores report how much different students know about the course content, they tell nothing for certain about when, where, and how they learned it. It is thus theoretically possible that the students learned all they knew *before* they took the course. In general, this method of evaluating a training program is the most naive and the least defensible.[10]

---

[9] The control group may become an experimental group (participate in training) *after* it has served as a control group. This is discussed later in this chapter.

[10] Smith, *op. cit.,* 309.

In this situation, nothing is available against which to compare criteria, the indices of change. Even if participants score "high" on a test of knowledge or satisfaction, there is no way to say how they got there. Conceivably, they may even have been higher on a measure of satisfaction *before* development!

The point, of course, is that this procedure defeats the concept of "change." Inherent in change is comparison, and no comparison is possible. The best that can be hoped for is that something can be learned about 1) the "state of affairs," where our participants fall on our criteria, or 2) how they feel toward the development effort which, in actuality, may be just another aspect of the "state of affairs."

What if the criterion measurements are taken *before and after* the development program, still without a control group? Here we can demonstrate change through a comparison of the "before" and the "after" measures. The magnitude and direction of change can be assessed. Is this sufficient? If you are interested in the effect of development, the answer is an emphatic "no!" For the question this approach cannot answer is: "Were the changes due to the development effort?" There is virtually no way to be certain whether or not they were. Such changes may have occurred in a group which did not undergo training, or perhaps factors extraneous to the development effort account for the results. The extent to which this is true, of course, depends upon the nature of the criterion and the intention and content of development. Before and after measures without a control group are defensible when the aim is to compare *methods* of training. Differences between the methods can be assessed; the group exposed to Method A may change considerably *more* on a criterion than the group exposed to Method B. Scores on the "before" measures are the basis for computing change, and the amount of change for each method is easily compared. Their experiences and characteristics, however, must be similar, and differences must lie mainly in the method of training.

What if Control Groups Are Used?

Suppose criterion measures are taken only *after* training, but we have one group that participates in the training *and* one which does not. In this situation, we are approaching better evaluation. Why? First of all, comparisons can be made. If, for example, the control group is much lower on a test of knowledge than the experimental group to whom this knowledge was imparted, it is a justifiable inference that the development had an impact. And if the knowledge seems to pay off in a second criterion measurement taken six months after development (e.g., increased productivity for the experimental group and no change in productivity for the control group), the inference is reinforced.

But a weakness still exists. The procedure assumes that the experimental group and the control group were the same *before* development. This is another way of saying that *comparisons* can be made, but *changes* cannot be assessed. Alternative explanations for the results exist, and the effects of the development effort may be omitted from these explanations. For example, the experimental group may have been higher or better on the criterion before training. It may, furthermore, have been on an "improvement trend" before training and the training served primarily as a reinforcement. Or, conversely, it may have been worse before training and had more "room" to improve regardless of training. In this latter case, the development effort could have effected a substantial change without appearing to if the experimental group improved only to a point below or at the level of the controls. Hence, conclusions about the effect of development carry with them some degree of risk concerning their accuracy. Again, a great deal depends on the nature of the criterion, and the changes one would reasonably expect given the conditions of development.

One way to reduce the risk of erroneous conclusions is to insure the similarity of the experimental and control groups on those factors entering into the evaluation of development. This similarity can be accomplished through random assignment of managers to each group. Here, their similarity should be analyzed and reported as part of the results of evaluation. Another way to insure comparability is to systematically assign people to groups. If, then, the groups are alike regarding age, productivity indices, years of service with the organization, etc., then differences can more reasonably be attributed to development.

By far the best experimental design is one in which measures are taken both before *and* after development, using *both* experimental *and* control groups. The design is as follows:

Groups	Pre-development	Development	Post-development
Experimental	Criteria measured	Yes	Criteria measured
Control	Criteria measured	No	Criteria measured

In this design, comparisons can be made, and changes demonstrated. And if the difference in the two groups results solely from exposure to development, a true evaluation situation exists. Changes which occur in the experimental group can be compared to changes in the control group. That is, if any extraneous factors produce changes in the criteria, these will be reflected in control group changes. The error of attributing these changes to the development effort can be overcome. Naturally, attempts should still be made to prevent differential effects not associated with the development program from occurring. Predevelopment matching of the two groups can help overcome beginning differences, while as stated earlier, group similarities and differences should be examined and reported.

Whenever possible, this is the design to be used if maximum information and adequate evaluation are to be attained. Every effort should be made, therefore, to include control groups in evaluation plans and procedures.

Are There Any Problems in the Use of Control Groups?

A problem exists in the use of control groups in that measurements taken on these groups at two points in time without any training might well incur resentment and antagonism on their part. McGehee and Gardner,[11] propose a design to overcome this problem. They suggest informing the control group that they will participate in development at a later date. The design then becomes:

---

[11] W. McGehee and J. E. Gardner, "Supervisory Training and Attitude Change," *Personnel Psychology*, Vol. 8, No. 4 (Winter 1955), 449-460.

Groups	Pre-devel. (1)	Devel. (1)	Post-devel. (1)	Dev. (2)	Post-devel. (2)
Experim.	Measure	Yes	Measure	No	No
Control	Measure	No	Measure	Yes	Measure

This is a simple extension of the last design discussed above. In it, both groups undergo development, and the value of a control group with before and after measures is retained.

Solomon[12] has presented further extensions of these designs, using several control groups. These designs are aimed to meet some of the problems which result from using controls and from some of the more subtle aspects of experimental design and analysis. The reader is also referred to McGehee and Thayer[13] for an excellent coverage of these problems as well as of other aspects of development and its evaluation. Whatever the control group design, plans can always make provision for the maximum training of all groups involved.

One final word on design. A good design cannot compensate for poor criteria, just as good criteria cannot help a poorly designed evaluation. And despite the many considerations briefly dealt with here, the organization cannot be expected to benefit fully from development unless it commits itself to good evaluation.

In conclusion, let us enumerate some guides which, hopefully, will help to round out the evaluation picture.

Summary

The following is a summary of the basic guides which apply to the measurement of behavioral change, as revealed in a survey of the literature:[14]

1) Programs based on specific needs can more easily be evaluated.

2) Variables should be isolated and taken into consideration.

3) Assumptions and limitations should be clearly stated.

---

[12] R. L. Solomon, "An Extension of Control Group Design," *Psychological Bulletin*, Vol. 46, No. 2 (March 1949), 137-150.

[13] McGehee and Thayer, *op. cit.*

[14] R. J. House, "An Experiment in the Use of Selected Methods for Improving the Effectiveness of Communication Training for Management," unpublished Ph.D. dissertation (Columbus, Ohio: The Ohio State University, 1960).

4) Evaluation requires clear-cut operational definition of the conditions, methods, the program, and the purposes of the learning activity.

5) During the planning stages of the program provision should be made for evaluation to take place.

6) Evaluation should be continuous, systematic, and comprehensive.

7) Results of the investigation should be expressed in terms that are understandable to those involved.

8) The purpose of evaluation should be to improve the quality and character of the learning activity as well as to determine answers to specific questions connected with the development program.

CHAPTER 7

CONCLUSIONS AND FURTHER QUESTIONS

by Robert J. House

We have addressed this book to the practicing executive or the staff analyst concerned with managerial development and succession. In dealing with those managerial practices which lead to or hinder the development of managers, we have presented guidelines based on social science research related to the process of managerial learning or performance improvements.

In our view, the practice of management resembles, in some respects, the practices of medicine and engineering. All three professions, for example, use scientific methodology and findings to improve their practitioners' performance. Clearly, physicians (in their diagnosis of symptoms) and engineers (in their design of buildings) do not claim absolute precision; they must exercise judgment, as well as apply scientific methodology, in defining problems and diagnosing illnesses. In making judgments, aid is sought from several disciplines: physicians, for example, call upon pharmacology, biology, chemistry, psychology, and other disciplines, while engineers call upon mathematics, physics, chemistry, electronics, and other physical sciences. In selecting the particular scientific information which applies to a given problem and in deriving prescriptions based on this information, both the physician and the engineer apply judgment, interpretation, and intuition, depending heavily upon what might be called an "artistic" ability.

We hold that the field of management is, no less than medicine and engineering, susceptible to the application of scientific principles. Through the application of the social sciences and mathematics, for example, it is possible to continually narrow the range of uncertainty in managerial decisions; and, like medicine and engineering, the practice of management will never be a purely scientific effort since there will always be a need for managers to interpret situations to be managed, and to temper the use of scientific principles in order to predict the consequences of events.

It is from this perspective that recommendations in previous chapters have been advanced. We believe that when the organizational conditions support the development effort, a manager will be significantly more likely to transfer the learning effort to his job. Knowledge of the nature and operation of the climate factors will, furthermore, help managers determine appropriate strategies for their own efforts. We would be unwarranted, however, in making any claim concerning the scientific probabilities which are associated with the presence or absence of specific motivating or reinforcing factors. Two reasons account for this hesitancy. First, the scientific identification and measurement of factors which determine or facilitate success in management development is a difficult and as yet unsolved problem; at best we can identify several such factors when they exist in rather large magnitudes. Under such conditions, a knowledge of previous science findings helps to design and implement development efforts. The second reason for this hesitancy is the assumption of *certeris paribus;* scientific predictions are possible only under those conditions in which a scientist can measure and thereby either account for, or control, contaminating forces or variables. By means of laboratory experiments, or by the use of environmental controls in field settings, it is possible for the social scientist to control forces and variables other than those under investigation. By replication of such experiments he may eventually arrive at principles which describe human reactions to certain stimuli, *assuming that other factors remain equal.*

One class of stimuli studied extensively by social scientists is what we have referred to as "development efforts." Repeated experimentation makes possible a statement such as, "If in the past the occurrence of a particular stimulus-situation has been the occasion on which a man's activity has been rewarded, then the more similar the present stimulus-situation is to the past one, the more likely he is to emit the activity or some similar activity now." This principle, a basic proposition in experimental psychology, implicitly assumes that all other factors will remain equal. For example, assume that a man finds himself in a stimulus-situation similar to one that has been rewarding to him in the past. At the same time, he is aware of threats of punishment if he emits the activity for which he has been rewarded in the past. Here we have a situation in which the other forces in the environment do not remain either neutral or equal. Consequently, one might argue that the social science principle is invalid. We would argue to the contrary.

For its valid application, knowledge is required of both the principle and the environment in which it is to be applied. But a knowledge of the environment rests upon one's personal ability to perceive other factors around him and to estimate how these factors are related to the problem. A knowledge of social science findings can help one to recognize variables which have been studied scientifically and about which predictions can be made. However, since both the environment and the job of management are constantly changing, it is unlikely that the manager will be very able to rely completely on the applications of scientific principles. Rather, it is more realistic to say that less interpretation will be required if he is aware of such principles.

This book has attempted to utilize the results of social science research in analyzing problems of management development. A review of the literature, however, discloses more issues and questions than explanations or prescriptions. In the following section we will discuss some of these issues and their implications for management.

Some Unresolved Issues

What Makes a Good Manager?

We have assumed throughout this book that the practicing manager is able to define the kind of managerial behavior required for effective performance. Our argument is essentially as follows: Once the desired managerial performance and the individual changes required to achieve this performance have been specified, we must provide not only a learning mechanism, but also conditions which motivate and reinforce the manager involved in development. On the basis of this assumption, we have proceeded to discuss in some detail 1) methods appropriate for changing the knowledge levels, attitudes, skills, and performance of managers, and 2) recommendations for providing the necessary motivations and organizational reinforcements. In other words, the methods suggested are those which we think will facilitate the development and improvement of performance.

However, we have not squarely faced the question, "What makes a good manager?" In fact, we have deliberately skirted this issue. Instead we have said that top management must decide the kind of behavior it would like the management team to exhibit. From theory, observation, and research, several aspects of managerial behavior can be described which may or may not be susceptible to change. For example, managerial activities have been described by others as those of planning, organizing, and controlling; leadership behavior has been described along both an authoritarian and a democratic continuum; and, behavioral science research has identified such factors as consideration, initiation of structure, influence with superiors, and the application of such specific social skills as conference leadership, interviewing, counseling, and performance appraisal. There is little question that the body of knowledge concerning management and leadership has been continually growing. If development efforts are to yield improved managerial behavior, it is necessary to answer the question, "What kind of behavior is desirable for effective managerial performance?"

In Chapter 2 we attempted to suggest a method whereby managers might arrive at answers to this question for themselves and their particular organizations. However, the answers and the means we suggest to pursue them are far from adequate and hardly free from controversy.

Changing Behavior

An accurate statement of organizational objectives implies that the behavior required to achieve those objectives is desirable. If this is so, then deviation from these behavior patterns represents areas in which development is needed. One of the most impressive results from research is that managerial attitudes and performance have changed as a result of participation in development efforts. Little is known, however, about the particular categories of behavior most susceptible to change or about the ranges in which changes can be reasonably expected and efficiently achieved.

We need to become more familiar with the general impact of the various developmental methods. More particularly, these methods need to be examined in relationship to 1) the task, 2) the goals to be achieved, and 3) the characteristics of the individuals involved. It is clear that certain kinds of managerial skills (e.g., interviewing, conference leading, the use of operation research techniques), can be effectively developed, but it is not readily apparent that they can be easily transmitted to the job situation.

Thus, there must be some provision for transfer of learning to the work environment. Resistance to change, both individual and organizational, must be overcome if transfer is to occur. Factors which preclude the transfer of learning reside partly within the individual learner and partly within the environment in which the new skills are to be applied. The extent to which initial managerial attitudes and established habits prohibit effective learning or prohibit transfer of training is as yet undetermined.

Attitude Change and Conformity

The ethics of change must also be examined. Many programs have attitude change as the major objective. To what extent is attitude conditioning desirable? Obviously, it is necessary for managers in an organization to work from essentially similar philosophical premises if teamwork and cooperation are to be achieved. However, a high degree of conformity may result in lower creativity and passive leadership. Is there no room for the insightful non-conformist? The manager who continually questions the "sacred cow" of the organization? Those who would cause us to take a second look? At what point does unity of attitude become uniformity of attitude? Under what conditions do conflicting beliefs result in fruitful discussion toward the identification of better alternatives? When is attitude change which reduces differences of opinions likely to yield stifling conformity in lieu of improved performance? Certainly the ethical considerations of change must not be cast aside. There appear to be no easy answers.

Organization Culture and Climate

Certainly those involved in development realize that it does not occur in a vacuum. While formal instruction may take place in a classroom, the concepts must be transferred to the organization in which the individuals operate and function. We have discussed in an earlier chapter the implications of formal organizational factors in reinforcing and motivating development efforts. It is unreasonable to expect effective managerial practices, or change, without organizational conditions which are conducive to them.

These formal organizational factors act as constraints on acceptable managerial behaviors. If the taught behavior does not fall within the constraints, it is unlikely that transfer will occur.

Our earlier discussions stress the importance of consistency between the intent of development efforts and such factors as organizational planning, managerial selection, and appraisal and compensation practices. However, there are undoubtedly many other aspects of the environment which affect the development process. Our knowledge of the elements and requirements of a developmental climate is far from complete. We are only beginning to learn how to describe some of the factors which constitute a developmental environment. Much remains to be discovered about the exact environmental factors which condition the effects of development efforts and how these factors can be conditioned to insure success.

What is a conducive climate? Certainly it is one in which the manager has the opportunity to utilize in practice those ideas presented in training; one in which the policy framework, the reward system and the leadership expectations are consistent with the content of the learning effort. It is this concept of organization culture and climate which is perhaps most important in transferring information and skills from training to the job. The organization conditions must be "right" or transfer will not occur. Management development programs can be and are often conducted outside the organizational environment but practices must be implemented within that environment if development is to succeed.

We have outlined one approach to conditioning the organizational climate. Undoubtedly, there are other less expensive and less time-consuming approaches. Our recommendations are based on inferences we have drawn from social science literature. We have taken a rather conservative approach by recommending that, in dealing with problems at hand, managers apply all resources which seem pertinent. One might legitimately question whether the suggested amount of time, effort, motivation, and reinforcement is actually required to do the job. One might also ask whether our approach is even reasonable in light of the tremendous demands, both financial and time-wise, imposed on top management. Clearly, we have much to learn about how to accomplish development without undue expenditures of time, effort, and money.

Criteria to Evaluate Development

To answer the questions raised above, and to determine whether management development efforts are yielding desired results, it is necessary to evaluate the effectiveness of such efforts. We have argued that development should be evaluated in terms of its effect on managerial performance. But the design and implementation of evaluation systems which both measure and identify causes of managerial performance change is a very expensive and time-consuming process. Indeed, rigorous evaluation of managerial development efforts may be as expensive as the effort itself. How, then, can the manager evaluate development? Can he afford to assume that the method being employed is actually giving him the kind of changes desired? To what extent can he rely upon such evidences as post-learning testimony, the logic of the approach, and his own observations? To what extent should he endeavor to obtain more systematic and empirical evidence of change?

To date most of the social science research concerned with management performance has been conducted by university faculty and sponsored by foundations, government agencies, and university endowments. As a result, the findings have been fragmentary and, at best, only suggestive of the potential contribution which could be made if such research were conducted on an organized and focused basis. However, the past five years have witnessed what may be the beginning of a trend in which business itself sponsors this kind of research. A few large organizations have established social science research staffs for the purpose of scientifically studying the effects of development programs and activities within the organization. Although such efforts are still in their infancy, they provide us with reason to believe that they will become not only financially self-supporting, but also, and eventually, even profitable.

It is our belief that continued inquiry will begin to answer the questions raised in this chapter and to provide an increasingly more systematic and predictable basis for those activities intended to improve the level of management performance. It is our hope that this book will provide additional and continuing impetus in the use of an empirical approach to management development.

APPENDIX I

"Manager Development: A Conceptual Framework, Some Propositions and Imperatives"

by Robert J. House

1. *PURPOSE AND SCOPE*

In 1957, Professor Phillip Selznick maintained that

> The whole problem of leadership training, and more generally of forming and maintaining elites, should receive a high priority in scientific studies of organization and policy. (1957, p. 15)

This appendix presents one effort toward making the study and practice of management development more of a technology or an applied social science. We first review previous research dealing with the conditions under which management development efforts are most likely to be effective, ineffective, or conflict-inducing. Secondly, we offer a taxonomy and a set of preliminary propositions intended to suggest how the objects to be investigated seem to hang together. Such an explanation is admittedly premature for the state of the art. Nonetheless, an attempt will be made to integrate and systematize the previous research so that subsequent investigations may be less fragmentary and more fruitful.

The content of this appendix is based primarily on a survey of empiric social science and business research pertinent to the process of management development. With few exceptions, the findings and conclusions disclosed in the literature survey were used only if they were based on studies meeting the minimum requirements of acceptable social science research; i.e., only if the research design provided for isolation, observations, and measurements of variables. When research not meeting these requirements is cited, an attempt is made to note any deficiencies in research method and to qualify conclusions accordingly.

2. *DEFINITION OF MANAGEMENT DEVELOPMENT*

For purposes of this appendix we shall define as management development any planned effort to improve current or future manager performance by imparting information, conditioning attitudes, or increasing skills. This definition implies that the results of development must be defined in terms of measurable change in either learner states or learner performance.

3. DEVELOPMENT VERSUS ALTERNATIVE METHODS FOR INDUCING CHANGE

If development *is* managerial change, how does this kind of change differ from change resulting from other causes? Change can, of course, be effected by a variety of other methods: (a) replacement of poor performers; (b) imposition of controls such as budgets, restrictive procedures, or close supervision; (c) realignment of position responsibilities and reorganization of individual job assignments; (d) use of participative decision making to gain group or individual acceptance; (e) bargaining; (f) outright coercion, either social or physical.

The essential difference between management development and other methods of inducing change is that development requires primarily a change of *attitude and understanding;* whereas these elements are usually not fundamental to the other types of change.

Thus management development is viewed here as one alternative for accomplishing organizational change.

4. ASSUMPTIONS

The studies upon which this paper is based, and therefore the situations to which it applies, are those in which a set of persons in an organization is assigned the task of changing particular behavior pattern(s) of designated members of the organization. Thus, at a given time, the organization is made up of two subsets of persons: change agents and learners.

We consider the set of persons at time t_0. Prior to this time, the change agent specified the participants in the development effort, and the objectives, content, and methods of the development effort. We deal with efforts to change individual learners' knowledge, attitudes, skills, and performance through planned learning processes.[1]

5. THE VARIABLES — TAXONOMY AND DEFINITIONS

For purposes of clarification and analysis, we classify the major factors suggested by previous studies into four categories: 1) objectives of the development effort; 2) initial learner states; 3) initial organizational states; and 4) developmental methods of inducing learner change. The developmental methods serve as the stimuli, or input, variables; the objectives of the development effort are the output variables. The initial state variables are moderators that interact with the development methods to influence the outputs.

5.1 Objectives of the Development Effort

The determination of desired terminal behavior is a prerequisite for deciding what methods will be employed to achieve desired behavior on the part of an individual learner. In other words, we assume the objectives of management development have been specified in operational terms (Mager, 1962).

---

[1] We do not deal with efforts to change group or organizational behavior.

The objective of management development may be a desired level of the learner's knowledge, a desired attitude of the learner toward the job practices taught in the development program, a desired skill level of the learner, or a desired performance level of the learner on his current job. Thus, the objectives of the management development effort can be defined as a desired terminal state, at time t_n, in any one, or more, of the following categories.

Knowledge: Knowledge objectives prescribe responses that a learner is expected to make in reply to questions about the material taught in the program.

Attitudes: Objectives concerned with attitudes prescribe the stand or the conviction that the individual is expected to uphold relative to the prescriptions taught in the learning phase of the development effort.

Skill: Objectives concerned with achievement of skill or development of latent abilities prescribe the overt responses that a learner is *expected* to exhibit under training conditions. Skill objectives may be classified into three broad categories: intellectual, manual, and social. As used here, the term skill refers to the learner's ability to recognize (discriminate) and respond to stimuli in the manner prescribed in the knowledge phase of the development effort. Ability to respond correctly in a learning situation, although a measure of skill, does not guarantee a change in job performance.

Job Performance: Performance objectives prescribe desired response to actual job situations and problems, rather than training situations.

5.2 Initial Conditions

The initial conditions under which change is initiated can be described in terms of two classes of variables: the initial state of the learner and the initial state of the environment in which the learner performs his position duties.

5.21 Initial State
of the Learner

We may conceptualize the state of the learner as consisting of four variables associated with successful participation in development efforts. These are:

¶ The discrepancy between (a) the initial state of the learner's knowledge, attitude, skill, and job performance, and (b) the desired terminal state

¶ The learner's adaptability

¶ The learner's ability to learn

¶ The learner's ego involvement with the prescriptions taught in the learning phase of the development effort.

The rationale or research relative to each of the above variables is briefly reviewed in the following section.

5.211 *Discrepancy Scores*

The discrepancy between the desired state and the initial state of the learner indicates the amount of necessary change; thus, the greatest possible discrepancy occurs when the difference between the initial and desired learner states is greatest. With the exception of attitude discrepancies,[2] we would expect the greatest change to take place in those learners for whom the difference between the initial and desired states is greatest—assuming adequate ability to learn and ability to adapt to new behavior patterns. Where ability to learn is insufficient for mastery of the information taught in the learning phase of the development effort, or where established responses are so ingrained that change requires extinction of responses, we would expect little change.[3]

5.212 *Adaptability*

By adaptability is meant the components of the learner's general ability to change, or the degree to which an individual is generally able to relinquish previously established modes of responding to a task situation and to adopt new, more varied modes of response. Thus, the degree to which the learner has established *behavioral responses* to stimuli involved in the prescriptions taught in the learning effort is an inverse function of his adaptability. As we conceive it, adaptability does not include the learner's specific attitude toward the prescriptions taught in the development effort, but only his ability to change behavioral responses.

5.213 *Ability to Learn*

The common-sense notion that a person's native ability affects his learning performance has been amply investigated. Numerous studies have been conducted to determine the effect of IQ, verbal ability, and other abilities on academic or professional achievement. If, however, any clear conclusion can be drawn from this literature, it is that any direct relationship between ability and performance is greatly modified by other variables. Social influences (e.g., peer group attitude toward learning achievement) can greatly modify the extent to which an individual utilizes his capacity. The interaction of social influence and ability to learn will be considered below. For the present it is sufficient to recognize the mediating effect of social influences and to assert that ability to learn is positively related to acquisition of knowledge. Management development studies using standard intelligence tests support this view (Neel and Dunn, 1960; Savitt, 1957; Gruenfeld, 1960; Katzell, 1948).

---

[2] See section 5.214, below, for a discussion of this exception.

[3] We do not claim that change is impossible under such conditions, but that it is improbable: (a) The learner has already reached maturity and is therefore usually unwilling to go through training or therapy requiring abandoning old habits and reevaluating behavioral patterns that have become an integral part of his personality; (b) It is rare that organizationally sponsored development efforts provide for learning exercises directed primarily at extinguishing habits and responses.

5.214 *Ego Involvement*

There is substantial evidence to indicate that high ego involvement tends to prevent attitude modification. Charters and Newcomb (1952) point out that the extent to which value system and related attitudes are tied to the self-image is an important consideration in attempts to modify specific attitudes. Katz, Sarnoff and McClintock (1956), McClintock (1958), Culbertson (1957), Peak and Morrison (1958), and Neel and Dunn (1960) report findings that suggest that individuals who are low in ego defensiveness are likely to be more susceptible to attitude change; Sherif, Sherif, and Nebergall (1965) find that the absolute level of an ego involvement is inversely related to the amount of attitude change.

Ego Involvement vs. Attitude Discrepancy at t_0

There is earlier research concerned with the use of measures of discrepancy between the learner's initial attitudes and the content of the change communication as a predictor of change resulting from the change communication. Fisher and Lubin (1958) and Whittaker (1965) report experiments suggesting that this relationship can be plotted as a unimodal (inverted V) curve. In other words, when the discrepancy between the change agent attitude and the learner's attitude is at midpoint, the amount of change will be greatest; when the discrepancy either rises or falls, the amount of change decreases. These findings, plus common-sense observation, support this notion. For when the discrepancy is highest one would *expect* a high degree of resistance, and therefore little attitude change; when discrepancy is lowest little attitude change would be necessary, and a ceiling effect would obtain. Ward (1965) has shown experimentally and by subject selection that the more ego-involved the subject, the more he will view a change communication as discrepant from his own position. Thus ego involvement and attitude discrepancy are not independent of each other. We see ego involvement or discrepancy as predictors of attitude change. However, one can obtain measures of ego involvement without the respondent being aware of the attitudes being tapped (Sherif, Sherif, and Nebergall, 1965). Such measurement is therefore likely to be a more reliable predictor than discrepancy measures which generally are based on questionnaire responses.

5.215 *Motivation to Learn*

The participant's perception of the potential and probable rewards to be gained as a result of changing his initial state constitute an important determinant of the effects of the development effort. Motivation to learn is primarily based on the personal and occupational needs of the learner and on his estimate of the benefits to be derived from the learning process. Thus, the more he perceives change in behavior to have personal advantage, the more he will be motivated to learn. Mowrer (1950) and McGeoch and Irion (1952) present reviews of experimental literature pointing out the importance to learning expectations, and show that when the learner expects to benefit from learning, he will learn more readily. Underwood and Richardson (1956) found a significant positive relationship between perceived salience of content and the individual's motivation to learn.

Unfortunately, there has been little research to suggest individual (as opposed to social) determinates of motivation to learn task-related information, or the kinds of incentives most likely to stimulate learning interest or effort. We would expect that individual managers would differ widely in their motivations. For example, it is likely that development opportunities are viewed by some managers as an opportunity for learning skills that are instrumental in the attainment of specific goals, thus rewarding because of the expectation that this will lead to specific occupational achievements or to the attainment of specific personal goals; and and that others view development as a self-actualizing event, rewarding because of the satisfaction experienced in the development process per se. Obviously, optimal design of development efforts requires a better knowledge of the motivations of the participants of the development efforts, and an adequate theory of development requires hypotheses concerning the relationship between motivations, learning, and transfer of training into improved managerial performance. At present there are few data to suggest such hypotheses.

5.22 Initial State of the Organizational
Environment — Social Influence Variables

Based on a review of literature pertinent to management development, Mann (1957) concludes that "The findings of these...studies suggest that trainers, researchers, and others interested in social change need to rethink what forces are necessary to create and sustain changes in orientation and behaviors with people in complex systems of relationships..." (p. 156).

Our own review confirms Mann's conclusion and suggests three broad classifications for the social influences in the managerial environment:

¶ The formal authority system of the organization

¶ The exercise of formal authority

¶ The primary group

Assessment of the initial environmental conditions makes it possible to estimate the source and amount of resistance to change that can be expected. Thus, assessment of the environment will suggest where antecedent conditions can be manipulated or conditioned to increase the probability of attainment of development objectives.

Each of the above three sources of social influence could act upon the learner in any of three ways. First, they may serve as antecedent conditions that motivate the learner to learn the necessary information, adopt the necessary attitudes, and exhibit the desired job performance. Second, they may act as a set of constraints on behavioral or performance change. Third, they may serve as reinforcements for achieving desired changes in knowledge, attitudes, skills, and performance.

The following is a description of how these three social influences have been found to relate to the effects of development effort.

5.221 *The Formal
      Authority System*

The formal authority system consists of the philosophy, practices, and precedents of policy-making executives. It is usually expressed in the form of administrative documents: organizational objectives, policies, procedures; organization charts; job descriptions; standards of performance; control systems; or the legitimized tradition of management practices.

There is some evidence, based on both survey research in natural field settings (Comrey, Pfiffner, and High, 1954) and laboratory experimentation (Pepinsky, Pepinsky, Minor, and Robin, 1959), that formal organizational practices influence organizational effectiveness. Field experimental evidence has shown that formal organizational practices affect managerial attitudes (Lieberman, 1954), as well as management development endeavors (Sykes, 1962; Hariton, 1951; Mann, 1957; House, 1960).

The study by Sykes, briefly described on pages 2 and 3, Chapter 1, dramatically illustrates the impact of the formal organization upon a management development program.

Sykes states that in this case the course created expectations for change that senior management was not willing to meet. The course brought about changes in the participants' perceptions of management's role. These changes in perception resulted in conflict between the formal authority system and the attitudes of learners.

5.222 *The Exercise of Formal Authority*

The exercise of formal authority is carried out by the learner's superiors, who exercise the right to administer rewards and punishments. The most influential superior is usually the one in hierarchical structure to whom the learner reports directly. There is evidence from survey research to demonstrate that subordinates tend to: act as their superiors act (Kahn and Katz, 1953; Katz, Maccoby, and Morse, 1950); possess attitudes similar to those of their superiors (Shills and Janowitz, 1948; Trumbo, 1961; Spector, Clark, and Glickman, 1960); and act in response to their perception of their superior's desires (Rosen, 1961). These findings pertain to military, government, and industrial settings. Thus we hypothesize that the superiors of the learner, through their exercise of formal authority, influence not only how their subordinates believe and behave, but also how subordinates respond to participation in development efforts. Studies concerned specifically with development efforts support this view (Meyer and Walker, 1961b; Rosen, 1961; Hariton, 1951; Triandis, 1958; Fleishman, Harris, and Burtt, 1955).

5.223 *The Primary Group*

The primary group of the learner consists of those organizational members who have frequent face-to-face contact with the learner. There is substantial evidence that the primary group is also capable of exerting significant influence on its members (Trumbo, 1961; Katz and Lazarsfeld, 1955; Murphy, Murphy, and Newcomb, 1937; Newcomb, 1943; Argyle,

1957; Asch, 1951, 1952; Bennett, 1955; Brodbeck, 1956; Gordon, 1952; Gurnee, 1937; Hardy, 1957; Mouton, *et al.*; 1956).

5.23 *Dimensions of*
Organizational Environment

Research discloses three dimensions of organizational environment, important to the development process, that apply to the above three social influence variables. These three dimensions are: congruence, clarity, and anxiety. The power of each of the environmental variables to influence the learner is some weighted function of these three dimensions.

5.231 *Congruence between the values represented by the social influence variables and the intent of the development efforts:* such congruence can be identified by determining the degree to which the social influence variable rewards or punishes the learner for adopting the kind of behavior or attitudes prescribed in the development effort.

The formal organization consists of policies that determine both the basis for, and the limits of, rewards and punishments exercised by the learner's superiors. Such policies are concerned primarily with criteria for performance appraisal, promotion, and compensation; for the allocation of authority, status, and power; and for control and corrective purposes. By determining the congruence between these criteria and the intent of the development effort, one can arrive at one measure of social influence.

The leader exercises authority by means of his personal contact with the participant; by allocation of job authority and responsibility; by execution of appraisal criteria; and by assignment of desirable and undesirable tasks, learning experiences, privileges, and fringe benefits. Thus the congruence between the leader's exercise of authority and the intent of the development effort is also a measure of social influence.

Finally, the primary group exercises reward and punishment pressures by means of norm enforcement. Thus congruence between group norms and prescribed behavior is also important when predicting learner expectations and change.

5.232 *Clarity of the relationship between the reward and punishment system and the intent of the development effort:* the degree of clarity partially determines the effectiveness of the social influence variables. The more the reward and punishment mechanisms are apparent and obviously related to changes intended to result from the development effort, the more effective they will be. Studies by Raven and Rietsema (1957) and by Georgopoulos *et al.* (1957) have shown that where the path toward the achievement of goals is not clear, goal achievement is significantly less probable. Stogdill (1959) reviews substantial literature that shows clarity of group norms to be positively related to the degree to which behavior is influenced by such norms.

5.233 *Threat, conflict, and anxiety-inducing properties of the environment:* there is a substantial body of literature that indicates learning efficiency and effectiveness are impaired under conditions where the learner experiences high levels of anxiety.

The presence of anxiety or frustration in a subject has been shown to lower problem-solving efficiency (Mukhopadhyay and Malani, 1960); make acceptance of new material less likely (Robbins, 1963); and interfere with overall performance (Feldhusen, 1965; Paul, 1964; and Solkoff, 1964); to make attitudinal changes less effective and enduring (Peterson and Thurstone, 1938; Cooper and Dinerman, 1951; Peregrine, 1936; Hall, 1938; Remmers and Morgan, 1936; Rosen, 1948; Chen, 1936; Hovland, Lumsdaine, and Sheffield, 1949; Rose, 1948; and Bettelheim and Janowitz, 1950); to lower efficiency of response to standarized tests (Feldhusen, 1965; Paul, 1964; Solkoff, 1964; and Beam, 1955); to lower memory accuracy (Wallen, 1942); and to reduce the appropriateness of behavioral responses (Barker, Dembo, and Lewin, 1941).

The social influence variables of our model are capable of inducing participant anxiety resulting from inconsistent policies, punitive, threatening leadership, and organizational conflict. When the learner views the policies or the exercise of such policies by his superiors as unfair and inconsistent; or, when organizational conflict or uncertainty concerning the consequences of his acts is so high that anxiety is induced; we hypothesize that learning efficiency, as well as the carry-over of knowledge, attitudes, and skills into job performance, will also be impaired.

5.24 *Some Questions About*
      Social Influence Variables

While the above studies demonstrate the importance of considering social influence variables in the design of development efforts and in the formulation of a theory to explain and predict the outcome of development efforts, they contribute little to our understanding of the sociological or psychological processes involved.

It appears that the three categories of social influences contain variables that may operate as necessary antecedent conditions, as intervening variables, or as reinforcers *after* knowledge, attitude, and skills change have occurred.

Kelman (1958) postulates that behavioral change can reflect any of three underlying social influence processes — compliance, identification, or internalization — and that the specific change process that occurs in development efforts will determine the amount of change, the intensity of the change, and its permanence.

The kind of influence process that operates, according to Kelman, depends on the kinds of influence the change agent possesses. French and Raven (1959) have advanced a taxonomy of the bases of social power (influence), all of which may exist to some degree in the managerial environment. They conceive of social power based on (a) the subject's belief in the agent's ability to reward or coerce the subject, (b) the subject's belief in the moral legitimacy of the influence acts by the change agent, (c) the subject's desire for identification with the change agent (referent power), or (d) the subject's perception of the influence agent as a possessor of knowledge (expert power) or skills in a particular area.

The three categories of social influences that we describe (the formal authority system, the exercise of formal authority, and the primary group) may be activated through processes similar to those hypothesized by Kelman. In so doing, these social influences may be based on any of the sources of power described by French and Raven.

Until more is known about the change mechanisms operating, it will be impossible to predict the circumstances and the stimuli that result in the most efficient and lasting change.

6. DEVELOPMENT EFFORTS

There are various methods for inducing change in level of learner knowledge and skill and in learner attitudes and job behavior. For example, leader-centered and student-centered discussion methods, case studies, role playing, management games, job rotation, feedback of performance appraisal information, selected reading and problem exercises have all been used as forms of developmental efforts. There is a growing body of empirically derived information relative to the kinds (but not the degrees) of developmental efforts that facilitate the initiation of change in managerial knowledge, attitudes, skills, and job performance states. The present section consists of a review of this information and an admittedly speculative description of how various kinds of manipulation affect change in learners. The methods reviewed here are not intended to suggest an exhaustive list of methods for inducing change in learner states; rather, this review suggests sets of manipulative techniques that have been shown by previous research to possess a statistically significant probability of influencing each of the learner states. The particular manipulations may simultaneously affect more than one learner state variable. Therefore, the effects of the manipulation are not mutually exclusive.

6.1 Methods Related to Knowledge Change

Change in the level of learner knowledge has been successfully induced by use of both permissive-student-centered instruction techniques and structured-leader-centered techniques (Anderson, 1959),[4] but both laboratory and field experiments have shown that the leader-centered method is superior to the student-centered method for inducing knowledge change

---

[4] "When the teaching method consists of discussion leading of a highly permissive nature, it is termed a 'student-centered' method. When much greater control is in the hands of the instructor, the method is frequently called 'leader-centered'."

in task-oriented populations.[5] (Asch, 1951; Brim, 1958; Husband, 1949; Spence, 1928; Thistlewaite, deHaan, and Kamenetzky, 1955; Wispe, 1951.)

6.2 Methods Related to
Attitude Change

The method of presenting information has been shown by Kimble and Garmezy (1963) to affect attitudes. They consider that an attitude consists of both an informational, or cognitive, component and an emotional, or affective, component. Thus, by definition, information can be an element in attitude change, unless the learner is ego-involved in the subject of the communication. For example, Sykes (1964) has shown that hostile attitudes of workers toward foremen can be changed by the method of presenting information. Group discussion has been found to be superior to lecture, in studies reported by DiVesta (1954), Guthe (1945), Hare (1962), and Preston and Heintz (1949); role playing has been shown to be effective for inducing attitude and opinion change by Brunnelle (1954), Culbertson (1957), Janis and King (1954), Mann and Mann (1958), and Souerwine (1956); and changes in role assignment have been found to influence role incumbent attitudes toward specific managerial ideologies (Larke, 1955; Lieberman, 1954).

6.3 Methods Related to
Skill Change

Role-playing experiments also demonstrate that managerial skills can be improved by providing opportunities to practice new skills while the trainee is still in the classroom. Maier, Hoffman, and Lansky (1960) found that lectures and group discussion techniques followed by role playing, rather than lecture and discussion techniques alone, resulted in significantly greater skill in handling difficult human relations problems in an interview situation. Lawsche and Bolda (1958) found significantly greater skills in diagnosing filmed human relations incidents among trainees who engaged in role playing than among those who engaged in leaderless discussion, or among non-trained groups; and Maier and Hoffman (1960) found that role playing in discussion techniques significantly improved the quality of the discussion leaders' skills.

---

[5] Anderson's review of 49 experiments concerned with the effects of leader-centered versus student-centered instruction revealed that the leader-centered technique has more positive effects on managerial motivation to learn than does the student-centered technique. Anderson separated the 49 studies he reviewed into task-oriented groups such as industrial, military, and governmental administrators, and socio-emotionally-oriented groups such as fraternities or groups of therapeutic patients. Leader-centered instruction was found to stimulate more enthusiasm for learning among task-oriented groups, whereas student-centered instruction resulted in higher enthusiasm among socio-emotional groups. Studies concerned with managerial and adult learning lend further support to this conclusion (Bennett, 1956; Filley and Reignard, 1962; House, 1962; Page and McGinnies, 1959).

6.4 Methods Related to Performance Change

The group decision method and the utilization of feedback appear to be two promising approaches to the attainment of attitudinal and job behavior change.

In the group decision method, the instructor calls for a decision by the participants after group discussion takes place. The decision usually involves private or public commitment to practice of the prescriptions being taught. Several investigators have found this an effective method for inducing change in post-decision performance after the trainee has left the training situation (Lewin, 1947; Levine and Butler, 1952; Bennett, 1955; Schachter and Hall, 1952).

Studies by Mann (1957), Smith and Knight (1959), Pryer and Bass (1959), Leavitt and Mueller (1951), Haney (1963), Mahler (1957), Meyer and Walker (1961a, 1961b), and Goodacre (1963) show that when evaluations concerning performance quality and quantity are provided to persons performing complex problem solving or managerial tasks, this feedback assists them in the attainment of desired performance and in bringing about improvement.

The above studies concerned with development efforts suggest certain *kinds* of efforts that are useful in bringing about desired change in the learner states. At present there is little evidence or theory to suggest the *amount* or combination of efforts required and the interaction between them. How much development effort is required to achieve desired terminal behavior is an empiric question, the answer to which has yet to be established. Furthermore, the conditions under which each method is most appropriate remain yet to be explicated.

7. DYSFUNCTIONAL CONSEQUENCES

There is also evidence to suggest that the effects of development efforts are not always those desired. Field experiments have revealed changes resulting from development effort that are contrary to its objectives, such as role conflict (Fleishman, Harris, and Burtt, 1955); increased learner dissatisfaction, turnover, and grievances (Sykes, 1962); and undesirable communication practices (House, 1960). And, case observation (Bennis, 1963; Schein and Bennis, 1965; and Buchanan, 1964) and field experimentation (Underwood, 1965) reveal that T-Group training resulted in increased stress for the learner upon return to his job environment.

We conceive of two kinds of dysfunctional consequences resulting from development efforts: role conflict and general learner anxiety.

7.1 Situational Conflict

Such conflict occurs when a learner is confronted by an element of the environment (e.g., a rule of the formal authority system, a directive from a superior, or informal pressure from the primary group) that is contrary to an attitude the learner adopted as a result of participation in the development effort. Such conflict is termed situational conflict, because it is confined to the particular situations in which the manager comes into contact with elements of the formal authority system, immediate superiors, or primary group. It is conceivable that the learner will find that one element of his environment conflicts with an attitude prescribed in the development effort, while another supports a prescribed attitude. Thus, such conflict is particular to both specific attitudes and localized situations such as staff meetings, work-group setting, personal contact with the superior, etc.

7.2 General Anxiety

A general level of learner occupational anxiety results from the algebraic sum of the conflicting forces exerted upon him by the environmental elements. This form of conflict will affect the learner's overall personal adjustment to his job and to life. The general level of anxiety resulting from the algebraic total net conflict from environmental elements will result in learner stress and will be characterized by such symptoms as loss of sleep, worry, and psychosomatic illness; and reduction of job efficiency.

The specific effects of induced conflict on performance are not clear. Undoubtedly, there are amounts of conflict which are sufficient to disturb the equilibrium within an organization and thereby increase efforts toward or readiness for change. The same kind of conflict, in sufficiently large amounts, is likely to cause disruption and have deleterious effects on organizational performance and managerial health. The effects of conflict and the conditions under which such conflict is likely to be beneficial or harmful to the learner or the organization can only be speculated on at the present state of knowledge. Obviously such effects depend heavily on the emotional state of the learner, his cognitive and managerial style and the level of his knowledge and skill, as well as the state of the human relationships within the organization.

8. A CONCEPTUAL FRAMEWORK — VARIABLE CLUSTERS ASSOCIATED WITH THE OUTCOME OF DEVELOPMENT EFFORTS

Having defined and classified the variables that have some empiric claim as significant to the development process, we are now ready to integrate the variables into a conceptual framework and speculate about the relationships between them.

The studies reviewed above suggest certain variables that are associated with both successful and conflict-inducing development efforts. When viewed collectively the variables fall into five roughly defined clusters, or "syndromes," that appear to be associated rather consistently with five different outcomes. One might speculate that these clusters constitute sufficient conditions for causing the different outcomes of development efforts. Figure 3 shows, in abbreviated form, the variables in our taxonomy and the clusters associated with each of the five output variables.

The outputs are labeled at the top of the table. Below each of these outputs are the inputs associated with it. For example, those conditions listed in Column I are associated with knowledge achievement; Column I and those conditions listed in Column II are associated with attitude change.[6]

Clearly, Figure 1 does not represent a precise formulation of the relationships among the variables; rather, it represents our speculation concerning the conditions that are sufficient for making a prognosis (clinically, rather than scientifically) concerning the impact of development efforts under given conditions. Figure 4 represents our conception of the process through which most development efforts take the learner. Figures 3 and 4 represent our perspective of the current state of management development knowledge.

9. *EVALUATION OF CURRENT STATE OF THE ART*

Several criticisms can be leveled against this perspective. The following are some of the more obvious gaps in our perspective of management development:

¶ First, our attempt to establish a system for predicting the outcome of development efforts requires consideration-of so many variables that it is probably more conservative than necessary to predict specified outcomes. That is, if one wanted to either provide for or measure all of the variables included in our clusters, he would have to provide control for, or manipulate, far more variables than would likely be necessary to achieve desired results. Thus, our attempt to make some sense of the literature lacks the attribute of scientific parsimony.

¶ Second, the relative influence of each variable is not suggested in the slightest, nor are the conditions under which one variable is likely to offset the influence of others or to interact with other variables to enhance their effectiveness.

¶ Third, the degree of each variable required for the attainment of outputs cannot be inferred from either previous research or theory. Thus, there is little guidance for one who wishes to determine at what point in the development sequence adequate knowledge has been attained to facilitate either attitude or skills development, and at what point sufficient attitude or skills development has been attained to begin efforts toward changing performance.

¶ Fourth, the time sequence suggested in Figure 4 is neither logically necessary nor strongly suggested by previous studies. Although this sequence seems plausible, there is little evidence to suggest which sequence of changes is most likely to be more effective, less dysfunctional, or more efficient. And there is little attention paid in the literature to the conditions requiring different sequences or strategies to induce change through

---

[6] This table is not intended to imply a sequence for the attainment of the objectives; rather, it is intended merely to accommodate the variable patterns associated with development outcomes.

Figure 3.
A TAXOMONY OF MANAGEMENT DEVELOPMENT VARIABLES

Inputs

| | | *Outputs* | | | |
	I	II	III	IV	V
	Desired change in knowledge	Desired change in attitude	Desired change in skill	Desired change in job performance	Unintended conflict, anxiety, or frustration
Participant and group characteristics	Motivation to learn Sufficient IQ	Col. I Plus Low ego involvement in subject matter being taught	Col. II Plus Nonconflicting habits or personality traits	Col. III Plus	Insufficient IQ to attain knowledge objective or inability to develop skills to desired level.
Development effort	Direct method of instruction (programmed learning, lectures, films, readings, and so on) Competent instruction	Discussion of on-the-job applications and personal benefits	Practice of desired abilities Corrective training to extinguish undesirable habits and behavioral patterns	Opportunity for on-the-job practice of newly acquired abilities and for feedback of results.	
Exercise of authority by superior		Neutral or positive attitude of superior toward development	Superior's attitude and example consistent with desired change	Coaching, counseling, and periodic performance review by superior consistent with desired performance	Negative attitude or behavior of superior
Formal authority system		Goals, top-management philosophy, and policies consistent with learning phase		Philosophy, practices, and precedents of the policy-making executives consistent with desired manager performance	Conflicting elements of formal authority system, e.g., punishment for achieving desired change, constraining policies and procedures.
Primary work group		Cultural conditions and social beliefs consistent with desired attitudes		Primary group norms consistent with desired change	Conflicting primary group norms

development. Not only is there a lack of evidence based on systematic comparisons of the effects of different time orderings of instruction methods or different sequences for achieving changes in learner states — but there have been no studies that even measured all of the output variables specified in this paper. Thus, the divisions of outputs into five categories and the suggestion of a desirable time sequence for the attainment of the desired outputs is highly arbitrary and tenuous.

¶ Fifth, it is highly unlikely that all of the variables apply with the same weight to all of the different kinds of development efforts that managers may experience. For example, ego involvement may be highly important in predicting the effectiveness of human relations training, but may have little value for predicting the outcome of training concerned with analytic skills such as long-range planning or applied mathematics.

¶ Sixth, there are probably variables other than those cited in this paper that act quite as powerfully to induce or condition change, but these have not yet been suggested by previous research. In fact, one is struck by the lack of available theory suggesting either additional variables, interactions between variables, or the relative importance of those already in our framework.

¶ Finally, without exception, the evidence concerning antecedent or intervening variables deals with short- rather than long-term changes, and consequences of development effort measure no longer than two-year durations. Little evidence is available concerning the conditions required either for influencing choice of career patterns or increasing managerial motivation for long-range career planning and development. With only a few exceptions have there been measurements of the long-range consequences of development efforts on careers.[7]

10. *PROPOSITIONS*

Recognizing that any attempt to integrate the results of previous research into an interactive system is highly speculative and tentative, we advance a set of propositions intended to offer some systemization of previous, fragmentary findings.

Proposition 1. General proposition — the kind and degree of change resulting from any given management development effort is a function of three sets of variables: the initial learner state, the amount of development effort engaged in by the learner, and the elements of the organizational environment of the learner.

Proposition 2. For any given communication of information during the learning phase of the development effort, a change in knowledge will be positively related to (a) the learner's motivation to learn, (b) the learner's ability to learn, (c) the amount of development effort engaged

---

[7] Two exceptions to this statement are the studies conducted by Miner (1965) and McClelland (1965).

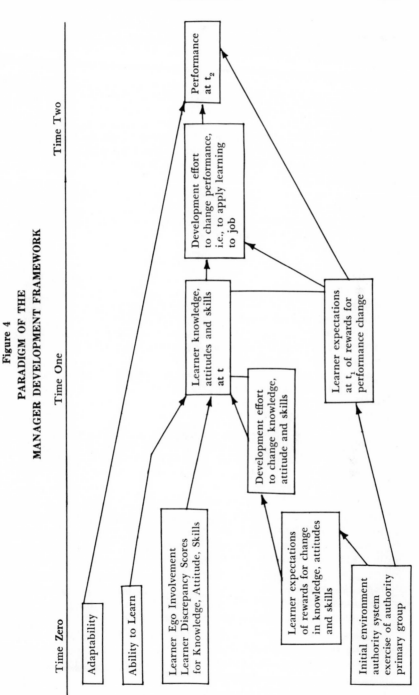

Figure 4
PARADIGM OF THE
MANAGER DEVELOPMENT FRAMEWORK

in by the learner to increase his knowledge, and (d) the learner's expectation that the knowledge advancement will be useful and rewarding to him.

Proposition 3. The learner's expectations of reward are dependent upon his perception of the potential reward to be gained as a result of (a) learning and (b) applying the prescriptions taught in the learning phases of the development effort. The learner's perceptions and expectations are determined by the degree to which the social influences within the organization are consistent with and supportive of both the intent and content of the prescriptions taught in the learning phases of the development effort.

Proposition 4. Assuming knowledge change has occurred, attitude change resulting from development efforts directed at attitudes will be inversely related to the learner's initial ego involvement in the content of the change communication and positively related to his perceptions of rewards for adopting new attitudes.

The learner's ego involvement is the degree to which he is committed *a priori* to attitudes concerning the prescriptions taught in the development effort. If he is highly committed *to the prescriptions* there will be little need for attitude change; his initial score will be high on the attitude scale; the prescriptions taught in the learning effort will merely reinforce his established attitudes; and his change will be limited by the upper boundary of the scale. Where the learner is committed to a contrary attitude, resistance will be high and change low, while the prescriptions taught in the learning phase may even alienate him. Where the learner is uncommitted, the probability of attitude change will be highest. Therefore, we postulate that attitude change will be inversely related to the absolute value of his ego involvement and positively related to his expectations of reward.

Proposition 5. After knowledge change has taken place, and given opportunity for practice and knowledge of the results of his practice efforts, changes in learner skills will be positively related to the learner's knowledge about the desired skills, his adaptability, his expectation that the achievement of such skills will be rewarded, and the discrepancy between his initial skill level and the desired one.

Proposition 6. Change in skill requires that the disutility involved in incurring the skill change (i.e., the costs involved in extinguishing old responses and habits and practicing the new skills) is not viewed by the learners as greater than the expected rewards for the achievement of the skill.

Proposition 7. Change in learner job performance is a function of change in learner skills, multiplied by changes in learner attitudes in interaction with the social influences in the environment at time t_1.

We view changes in skill as analogous to changes in individual ability to perform in a desired fashion. We view the social influence variables both as motivators to change behavior and as reinforcements for changed behavior. Previous research suggests that the relationships between these two sets of variables, ability and motivation, interact in a multiplicative way (reviewed by Vroom, 1964). Thus, we view the following two equations as analagous:

Performance = f (motivation) x (ability).

Performance = f (learner attitudes, environmental
social influences) x (learner skills).

Proposition 8. Situational conflict will occur in each situation in which the learner confronts a source of social influence that conflicts with his attitudes. He may experience localized conflict from his primary group, his superior, or from the formal authority system, when these environmental social influences are incongruent with the attitudes adopted by the learner as a result of the development effort.

Proposition 9. The general level of learner occupational anxiety is positively related to the algebraic sum of forces exerted on him from the the social influence elements of the organizational environment; and, assuming no change in social influences, changes in anxiety will result from changes in learner attitudes induced by the development effort.

11. *CONCLUSIONS: SOME IMPERATIVES*

This paper has advanced a conceptual framework for the process of management development and the major variables involved in this process — a framework derived from the empirical research available to date, thus representing a preliminary attempt to systematize previous findings. Following are some of the major implications to be drawn from this discussion:

1. The selection of learning content and teaching methods must be based on an analysis of the social influences in the learner's organization, as well as on learner needs. No two organizations require identical management practices, and hence no two organizations can effectively employ identical development content or methods.

2. Management development efforts, when conducted without due regard to environmental factors, may not result in improved management performance at all. Worse yet, such efforts may actually cause problems by inducing role conflict and management frustration.

3. When taken together, the studies concerned with participant characteristics imply that management development is not, and cannot be, a method for improving highly unhealthy organizations or highly malpracticing managers. These studies suggest that management development must be viewed as mental calisthentics useful for improving the already healthy manager, rather than as medicine for curing incompetence, lack of receptiveness, or negligence.

4. Previous disappointment with management development may be explained by the failure to consider the learner and organizational requirements for effective design and use of development methods. There is substantial evidence that well-conceived development efforts can induce desired changes in the managerial performance of the learner.

5. When it is determined that either the learner or his organization does not possess the initial qualities that predict successful development, other means of inducing change must be employed. Development is far from a panacea. It applies only under rather limited conditions. It is perhaps more realistically used in combination with other methods of inducing individual and organizational performance changes, such as managerial selection and replacement, job reassignment, reorganization, or the imposition of controls.

BIBLIOGRAPHY TO APPENDIX I

Anderson, R. C. "Learning in Discussions: A Resume of the Authoritarian-Democratic Studies." *Harvard Educational Review*, Vol. 29, Summer 1959, 201-215.

Argyle, M. "Social Pressure in Public and Private Situations." *Journal of Abnormal and Social Psychology*, Vol. 54, No. 2, March 1957, 172-175.

Asch, M. J. "Nondirective Teaching in Psychology: An Experimental Study." *Psychological Monographs*, Vol. 65, No. 4, 1951.

Asch, S. E. "Effects of Group Pressure Upon the Modification and Distortion of Judgments." H. Guetzkow, ed. *Groups, Leadership and Men.* New York: Russell & Russell, Inc., 1963, 177-190.

Asch, S. E. *Social Psychology.* New York: Prentice-Hall, Inc., 1952.

Back, K. W. "Influence through Social Communication." *Journal of Abnormal and Social Psychology*, Vol. 46, No. 1, January 1951, 9-23.

Barker, R. B., Dembo, T., and Lewin, K. "Frustration and Regression: an Experiment with Young Children." G. D. Stoddard, ed., "Studies in Topological and Vector Psychology II.", *University of Iowa Studies: Studies in Child Welfare*, Vol. 18, No. 1, 1941, 1-314.

Beam, J. C. "Serial Learning and Conditioning Under Real-Life Stress." *Journal of Abnormal and Social Psychology*, Vol. 51, No. 3, November, 1955, 543-551.

Bennett, E. B. "Discussion, Decision, Commitment and Consensus in 'Group Decision.'" *Human Relations*, Vol. 8, No. 3, August 1955, 251-273.

Bennett, W. E. "The Lecture as a Management Training Technique." *Personnel*, Vol. 32, No. 6, May 1956, 497-507.

Bennis, W. G. "A New Role for Behavioral Sciences: Effecting Organizational Change." *Administrative Science Quarterly*, Vol. 8, No. 2, September 1963, 125-165.

Bettelheim, B., and Janowitz, M. "Reactions to Fascist Propaganda: A Pilot Study." *Public Opinion Quarterly*, Vol. 14, No. 1, Spring 1950, 53-60.

Brim, O. G., Jr. *Sociology and the Field of Education.* New York: Russell Sage Foundation, 1958.

Brodbeck, M. "The Role of Small Groups in Mediating the Effects of Propaganda." *Journal of Abnormal and Social Psychology*, Vol. 52, 1956, 166-170.

Brunelle, P. "Exploring Skills of Family Life at School: Sonodrama with a Fourth-Grade Group." *Group Psychotherapy*, Vol. 6, No. 3-4, January-March 1954, 227-255; cited in R. Lippitt and A. Hubbell, "Role-Playing for Personnel and Guidance Workers: Review of Literature with Suggestion for Application," *Group Psychotherapy*, Vol. 9, No. 2, August 1956, 89-114.

Buchanan, P. C. "Evaluating the Effectiveness of Laboratory Training in Industry." Paper read at the American Management Association Seminar, New York, February 24-26, 1964.

Buchanan, P. C. "Factors Making for Effective Supervisory Training." *Personnel*, Vol. 34, No. 5, March-April 1958, 46-53.

Bunker, D. R. "Individual Applications of Laboratory Training." *Journal of Applied Behavioral Science,* Vol. 1, No. 2, April-May-June 1965, 131-148.

Carlson, E. R. "Attitude Change through Modification of Attitude Structure." *Journal of Abnormal and Social Psychology,* Vol. 52, 1956, 256-261.

Charters, W. W., Jr., and Newcomb, T. M. "Some Attitudinal Effects of Experimentally Increased Salience of a Membership Group." G. E. Swanson, T. M. Newcomb, and E. L. Hartley, eds., *Readings in Social Psychology,* rev. ed., New York: Henry Holt & Company, 1952, 1952, 415-420.

Chen, W. K. -C. "Retention of the Effect of Oral Propaganda." *Journal of Social Psychology,* Vol. 7, No. 4, November 1936, 479-483.

Chen, W. K. -C. "The Influence of Oral Propaganda Upon Students' Attitudes." *Archives of Psychology,* Vol. 23, No. 150, 1933.

Cohen, A. R. *Attitude Change and Social Influence.* New York: Basic Books, Inc., 1965.

Cohen, K. *The Role of Management Games and Education Research.* Unpublished Behavioral Theory of the Firm Working Paper No. 22, Carnegie Institute of Technology, Pittsburgh, 1962.

Comrey, A. L., Pfiffner, J. M., and High, W. S. "Factors Influencing Organizational Effectiveness." Los Angeles: University of Southern California (Mimeo), 1954.

Cooper, E., and Dinerman, H. "Analysis of the Film 'Don't be a Sucker': A Study in Communication." *Public Opinion Quarterly,* Vol. 15, No. 2, Summer 1951, 243-264.

Cronbach, L. J. "Processes Affecting Scores on 'Understanding of Others' and 'Assumed Similarity'." *Psychological Bulletin,* Vol. 52, No. 3, May 1955, 177-193.

Culbertson, F. M. "Modification of an Emotionally-Held Attitude through Role Playing." *Journal of Abnormal and Social Psychology,* Vol. 54, No. 2, March 1957, 230-233.

DiVesta, F. J. "Instructor-Centered and Student-Centered Approaches in Teaching a Human Relations Course." *Journal of Applied Psychology,* Vol. 38, No. 5, October 1954, 329-335.

Feldhusen, J. F., Denny, T., and Condon, C. F. "Anxiety, Divergent Thinking and Achievement." *Journal of Educational Psychology,* Vol. 56, No. 1, February 1965, 40-45.

Fiedler, F. E. "Leader Attitudes and Group Effectiveness." Monograph. Urbana: University of Illinois Press, 1958.

Filley, A. C., and Reighard, F. H. *A Preliminary Survey of Training Attitudes and Needs Among Actual and Potential Attendees at Management Institute Programs.* Madison: University of Wisconsin Press, November 1962.

Fisher, S., and Lubin, A. "Distance as a Determinate of Influence in a Two-Person Serial Interaction Situation." *Journal of Abnormal and Social Psychology,* Vol. 56, No. 2, March 1958, 230-238.

Fleishman, E. A. *Manual for Administering the Leader Opinion Questionnaire.* Chicago: Science Research Associates, 1960.

Fleishman, E. A., Harris, E. F., and Burtt, H. E. *Leadership and Supervision in Industry: An Evaluation of a Supervisory Training Program.* Columbus: The Ohio State University Press, 1955.

French, J. R. P. Jr., and Raven, B. "The Bases of Social Power." D. Cartwright ed., *Studies in Social Power,* Ann Arbor: University of Michigan, Institute for Social Research, 1959, 118-149.

Georgopoulos, B. S., Mahoney, G. M., and Jones, N. W., Jr. "A Path-Goal

Approach to Productivity." *Journal of Applied Psychology*, Vol. 41, No. 6, December 1957, 345-353.

Goodacre, D. "Stimulating Improved Management." *Personnel Psychology*, Vol. 16, No. 2, Summer 1963, 133-143.

Gordon, R. L. "Interaction between Attitude and the Definition of the Situation in the Expression of Opinion." *American Sociological Review*, Vol. 17, No. 1, February 1952, 50-58.

Gruenfeld, L. W. "Selection of Executives for a Training Program." *Personnel Psychology*, Vol. 14, No. 4, Winter 1960, 421-431.

Gurnee, H. "A Comparison of Collective and Individual Judgments of Fact." *Journal of Experimental Psychology*, Vol. 21, No. 1, July 1937, 106-112.

Guthe, C. E. *Manual for Study of Food Habits.* Report of the Committee on Food Habits, Bulletin of the National Research Council, No. 111, Washington, D.C.: 1945.

Hall, W. "The Effect of Defined Social Stimulus Material Upon the Stability of Attitudes Toward Labor Unions, Capital Punishment, Social Insurance, and Negroes." A. H. Remmers, ed., "Further Studies in Attitudes, Series 3," *Studies in Higher Education*, Vol. 34, 1938, 7-19, LaFayette, Indiana: Purdue University, The Division of Educational Reference.

Haney, W. "A Laboratory Experiment in Bilateral and Unilateral Communications." Paper presented at the Midwest Management Conference, Columbus, Ohio, April 1963.

Hardy, K. R. "Determinants of Conformity and Attitude Change." *Journal of Abnormal and Social Psychology*, Vol. 54, No. 3, May 1957, 289-294.

Hare, A. P. *Handbook of Small Group Research.* New York: The Free Press of Glencoe, 1962.

Hare, A. P. "Small-Group Discussions with Participatory and Supervisory Leadership." *Journal of Abnormal and Social Psychology*, Vol. 48, No. 2, April 1953, 273-275.

Hariton, T. "Conditions Influencing the Effects of Training Foremen in New Human Relations Principles." Unpublished Ph.D. dissertation, The University of Michigan, Ann Arbor, Michigan, 1951.

House, R. J. "An Experiment in the Use of Management Training Standards." *Journal of the Academy of Management*, Vol. 5, No. 1, April 1962, 76-81.

House, R. J. "An Experiment in the Use of Selected Methods for Improving the Effectiveness of Communication Training for Management," Unpublished Ph.D. dissertation, The Ohio State University, Columbus, 1960.

Hovland, C. I., Lumsdaine, A. A., and Sheffield, F. D. "Experiments on Mass Communication." *Studies in Social Psychology in World War II*, Vol. 3. Princeton, N.J.: Princeton University Press, 1949.

Hughes, E. C. "The Knitting of Racial Groups in Industry." *American Sociological Review*, Vol. 11, No. 5, October 1946, 512-519.

Husband, R. "A Statistical Comparison of the Efficiency of Large Lecture versus Smaller Recitation Sections upon Achievement in General Psychology." *American Psychologist*, Vol. 4, No. 7, July 1949, 216.

Janis, I. L., and King, B. T. "The Influence of Role Playing on Opinion Change." *Journal of Abnormal and Social Psychology*, Vol. 49, No. 2, April 1954, 211-218.

Jaques, E. *The Changing Culture of a Factory.* London: Tavistock Publications, 1951.

Jones, D. H., and Carron, T. J., "Evaluation of a Reading Development Program for Scientists and Engineers." *Personnel Psychology*, Vol. 18, No. 3, Autumn 1965, 281-295.

Kahn, R. L., and Katz, D. "Leadership Practices in Relation to Productivity and Morale." D. Cartwright and A. Zander, eds., *Group Dynamics: Research and Theory*. Evanston, Ill.: Row, Peterson & Company, 1953, 612-628.

Kahn, R. L., Wolfe, D. M., Quinn, R. D., and Snoek, J. D., in collaboration with R. A. Rosenthal. *Organizational Stress: Studies in Role Conflict and Ambiguity*. New York: John Wiley & Sons, 1964.

Katz, D., Maccoby, N., and Morse, N. C. *Productivity, Supervision and Morale in an Office Situation*. Ann Arbor, Michigan: Institute for Social Research, University of Michigan, 1950.

Katz, D., Sarnoff, I., and McClintock, C. "Ego-Defense and Attitude Change." *Human Relations*, Vol. 9, No. 1, February 1956, 27-45.

Katz, E., and Lazarsfeld, P. F. *Personal Influence: The Part Played by People in the Flow of Mass Communications*. Glencoe, Ill.: The Free Press, 1955.

Katzell, R. A. "Testing a Training Program in Human Relations." M. L. Blum, ed., *Readings in Experimental Industrial Psychology*. New York: Prentice-Hall, Inc., 1952, 64-70; and, *Personnel Psychology*, Vol. 1, No. 3, Autumn 1948, 319-329.

Kelman, H. C. "Compliance, Identification, and Internationalization: Three Processes of Attitude Change." *Journal of Conflict Resolution*, Vol. 2, No. 1, March 1958, 51-60.

Kidd, J. S., and Campbell, D. T. "Conformity to Groups as a Function of Group Success." *Journal of Abnormal and Social Psychology*, Vol. 51, No. 3, November 1955, 390-393.

Kimble, G. A., and Garmezy, N. *Principles of General Psychology*. 2nd Ed. New York: Ronald Press Company, 1963.

Lawshe, C. H., and Bolda, R. A. *Role Playing as an Industrial Leadership Training Technique*. LaFayette, Indiana: Organizational Research Center, Purdue University, 1958.

Lazarsfeld, P. F. "Forward" In H. Hyman, *Survey Design and Analysis: Principles, Cases and Procedures*. Glencoe, Illinois: The Free Press, 1957, 5-6.

Leavitt, H. J., and Mueller, R. A. H. "Some Effects of Feedback on Communication." *Human Relations*, Vol. 4, No. 4, November 1951, 401-410.

Levine, J., and Butler, J. "Lecture versus Group Discussion in Changing Behavior." *Journal of Applied Psychology*, Vol. 36, No. 1, February 1952, 29-33; also, D. Cartwright and A. Zander, eds., *Group Dynamics: Research and Theory*. Evanston, Illinois: Row, Peterson & Company, 1960, 280-286.

Lewin, K. "Lecture Compared with Group Decision (Red Cross Groups)." In "Studies in Group Decision," D. Cartwright and A. Zander, eds., *Group Dynamics: Research and Theory*. Evanston, Illinois: Row, Peterson & Company, 1960, 287-291. (A condensation of "Frontiers in Group Dynamics," *Human Relations*, Vol. 1. No. 1, February 1947, 5-41.)

Lieberman, S. "The Relationship Between Attitudes and Roles: A Natural Field Experiment." Unpublished Ph.D. dissertation, University of Michigan, Ann Arbor, 1954.

Mager, R. F. *Preparing Objectives for Programmed Instruction*. San Francisco: The Fearon Publishers, Inc., 1961.

Mahler, W. R. "Bringing About Change in Individual Performance." *Improving Managerial Performance*. New York: General Management Series, No. 186, The American Management Association, 1957.

Mahoney, T. A., Jerdee, T. H., and Korman, A. "An Experimental Evaluation of Management Development." *Personnel Psychology*, Vol. 13, No. 1, Spring 1960, 81-98.

Mahoney, T. A., Jerdee, T. H., and Nash, A. N. "Predicting Managerial Effectiveness." *Personnel Psychology*, Vol. 13, No. 2, Summer 1960, 147-163.

Maier, N. R. F. "The Quality of Group Decisions as Influenced by the Discussion Leader." *Human Relations*, Vol. 3, No. 2, June 1950, 155-174.

Maier, N. R. F., and Hoffman, L. R. "Using Trained 'Developmental' Discussion Leaders to Improve Further Quality of Group Decisions," *Journal of Applied Psychology*, Vol. 44, No. 4, August 1960, 247-251.

Maier, N. R. F., Hoffman, L. R., and Lansky, L. M. "Human Relations Training as Manifested in an Interview Situation," *Personnel Psychology*, Vol. 13, No. 1, Spring 1960, 11-30.

Mann, F. C. *Studying and Creating Change: A Means to Understanding Social Organization.* In C. M. Arensberg *et al.*, eds., *Research in Industrial Human Relations*, Vol. 7, New York: Harper, 1957, 68-103.

Mann, J. H., and Mann, C. H. "The Effect of Role Playing Experience on Self-Rating of Interpersonal Adjustment." *Group Psychotherapy*, Vol. 11, No. 1, March 1958, 27-32.

Mann, J. H., and Mann, C. H. "The Importance of Group Task in Producing Group-Member Personality and Behavior Changes." *Human Relations*, Vol. 12, No. 1, February 1959, 75-80.

McClelland, D. C. "Achievement Motivation Can Be Developed." *Harvard Business Review*, Vol. 43, No. 6, November-December 1965, 6-16, 20-24, 178.

McClintock, C. G. "Personality Syndromes and Attitudes Change." *Journal of Personality*, Vol. 26, No. 4, December 1958, 479-493.

McGeoch, J. A., and Irion, A. L. *The Psychology of Human Learning.* 2nd Ed. New York: Longmans, Green & Company, Inc., 1952.

Meyer, H. H., and Walker, W. B. "A Study of Factors Relating to the Effectiveness of a Performance Appraisal Program." *Personnel Psychology*, Vol. 14, No. 3, Autumn 1961, 291-298.

Meyer, H. H., and Walker, W. B. "Need for Achievement and Risk Preferences as They Relate to Attitudes Toward Systems and Performance Appraisal in an Industrial Setting." *Journal of Applied Psychology*, Vol. 45, No. 4, August 1961, 251-256.

Miles, M. B. "Changes During and Following Training: A Clinical Experimental Study," *Journal of Applied Behavioral Sciences*, Vol. 1, No. 3, July-August September 1965, 215-242.

Miner, J. B. *Studies in Management Education.* New York: Springer Publishing Company, 1965.

Mouton, J. S., Blake, R. R., and Olmstead, J. A. "The Relationship Between Frequency of Yielding and the Disclosure of Personal Identity." *Journal of Personnel*, Vol. 24, 1956.

Mowrer, O. H. *Learning Theory and Personality Dynamics: Selected Papers.* New York: The Ronald Press Company, 1950.

Mukhopadhyay, P., and Indira, M., "A Comparative Study of Natural and Emotive Sets as Conditions for the Blinding Effects on the Process of Productive Thinking." *Psychological Study*, Vol. 5, No. 2, 1960, 90-96.

Murphy, G., Murphy, L. B., and Newcomb, T. M. *Experimental Social Psychology.* Rev. Ed., New York: Harper & Brothers, 1937.

Neel, R. G., and Dunn, R. E. "Predicting Success in Supervisory Training Programs by the Use of Psychological Tests." *Journal of Applied Psychology*, Vol. 44, No. 5, October 1960, 358-360.

Newcomb, T. M. *Personality and Social Change.* New York: Dryden Press, 1943.

Page, R. H., and McGinnies, E. "Comparison of Two Styles of Leadership in Small Group Discussion." *Journal of Applied Psychology*, Vol. 43, No. 4, August 1959, 240-245.

Paul, G. L., and Eriksen, C. W. "Effects of Test Anxiety on 'Real-Life' Examinations." *Journal of Personality*, Vol. 32, No. 3, September 1964, 480-494.

Peak, H., and Morrison, R. W. "The Acceptance of Information into Attitude Structure." *Journal of Abnormal and Social Psychology*, Vol. 57, No. 2, September 1958, 127-135.

Pepinsky, H. B., Pepinsky, P. N., Minor, F. J., and Robin, S. S. "Team Productivity and Contradiction of Management Policy Commitments." *Journal of Applied Psychology*, Vol. 43, No. 4, August 1959, 264-270.

Pepinsky, P. N., Minor, F. J., and Robin, S. S. "Team Productivity as Related to the Confirmation or Contradiction by Management of its Commitments to an Appointed Leader." (Mimeo) Columbus: The Ohio State University, Personnel Research Board, 1957.

Peregrine, D. "The Effect of Printed Social Stimulus Material upon the Attitudes of High School Pupils Toward the Negro." H. H. Remmers, ed., "Further Studies in Attitudes, Series 2," LaFayette, Indiana: Purdue University, Division of Educational Reference, *Studies in Higher Education*, Vol. 31, 1936, 55-69.

Peterson, R. C., and Thurstone, L. L. *Motion Pictures and The Social Attitudes of Children*. New York: Macmillan, 1933.

Preston, M. G., and Heintz, R. K. "Effects of Participatory versus Supervisory Leadership on Group Judgment." *Journal of Abnormal and Social Psychology*, Vol. 44, No. 3, July 1949, 345-355.

Pryer, M. W., and Bass, B. M. "Some Effects of Feedback on Behavior in Groups." *Sociometry*, Vol. 22, No. 1, March 1959, 56-63.

Raven, B. H., and Rietsema, J. "The Effects of Varied Clarity of Group Goal and Group Path Upon the Individual and His Relation to His Group." *Human Relations*, Vol. 10, No. 1, February 1957, 29-45.

Remmers, H. H., and Morgan, C. L. "Changing Attitudes Toward a Racial Group." H. H. Remmers, ed., "Further Studies in Attitudes, Series 2." LaFayette, Indiana: Purdue University, The Division of Educational Reference, *Studies in Higher Education*, Vol. 31, 1936, 109-114.

Robbins, P. R. "Level of Anxiety, Interference Proneness, and Defensive Reactions to Fear-Arousing Information." *Journal of Personality*, Vol. 31, No. 2, June 1963, 163-178.

Rose, A. M. *Studies in Reduction of Prejudice: A Memorandum Summarizing Research on Modfication of Attitudes*. 2nd Ed. Chicago: American Council on Race Relations, 1948.

Rosen, H. "Managerial Role Interaction: A Study of Three Managerial Levels." *Journal of Applied Psychology*, Vol. 45, No. 1, February 1961, 30-34.

Rosen, I. C. "The Effect of the Motion Picture 'Gentleman's Agreement' on Attitudes Toward Jews." *Journal of Psychology*, Vol. 26, 1948, 525-536.

Savitt, M. A. "Is Managment Training Worthwhile?" *Personnel*, Vol. 34, No. 2, September-October 1957, 79-82.

Schacter, S., and Hall, R. "Group-Derived Restraints and Audience Persuasion." *Human Relations*, Vol. 5, No. 4, November 1952, 397-406.

Schein, E. H., and Bennis, W. G. *Personal and Organizational Change Througl Group Methods: The Laboratory Approach*. New York: Wiley, 1965.

Selznick, P. *Leadership in Administration: A Sociological Interpretation*. Evanston, Ill.: Row, Peterson & Company, 1957.

Sherif, C. W., Sherif, M., and Nebergall, R. E. *Attitude and Attitude Change* Philadelphia: W. B. Saunders Company, 1965.

Sherman, H. *Reducing Grievances Through Supervisory Training*. E. E. Jennings, ed. *Wisconsin Commerce Reports*, Vol. 3, No. 4, Madison: Bureau of Business Research and Service, University of Wisconsin, 1952.

Shils, E. A., and Janowitz, M. "Cohesion and Disintegration in the Wehrmacht in World War II." *Public Opinion Quarterly*, Vol. 12, No. 2, Summer 1948, 280-315.

Smith, E. E., Knight, S. S. "Effects of Feedback on Insight and Problem Solving Efficiency in Training Groups." *Journal of Applied Psychology*, Vol. 43, No. 3, June 1959, 209-211.

Solkoff, N., Todd, G. A., and Screven, C. G. "Effects of Frustration on Perceptual-Motor Performance." *Child Development*, Vol. 35, No. 2, June 1964, 569-575.

Souerwine, A., and Conway, K. "The Effects of Role-Playing Upon the Social Atmosphere of a Small Group of Sixth-Grade Children." Paper presented at the American Psychological Association Meeting, 1953; cited in R. Lippit and A. Hubbell, "Role-Playing for Personnel and Guidance Workers: Review of the Literature with Suggestions for Application." *Group Psychotherapy*, Vol. 9, No. 2, August 1956, 89-114.

Spector, A. J., Clark, R. A., and Glickman, A. S. "Supervisory Characteristics and Attitudes of Subordinates." *Personnel Psychology*, Vol. 13, No. 3, Autumn 1960, 301-316.

Spence, R. B. "Lecture and Class Discussion in Teaching Educational Psychology." *Journal of Educational Psychology*, Vol. 19, No. 7, October 1928, 454-462.

Stogdill, R. M. *Individual Behavior and Group Achievement: A Theory, The Experimental Evidence*. New York: Oxford University Press, 1959.

Stogdill, R. M., and Coons, A. E., eds. *Leader Behavior: Its Description and Measurement*. Columbus: Bureau of Business Research, College of Commerce and Administration, The Ohio State University, 1957.

Stotland, E., Thorley, S., Thomas, E., Cohen, A. S., and Zander, A. "The Effects of Group Expectations and Self-Esteem Upon Self-Evaluation." *Journal of Abnormal and Social Psychology*, Vol. 54, No. 1, January 1957, 55-63.

Sykes, A. J. M. "A Study in Changing the Attitudes and Stereotypes of Industrial Workers." *Human Relations*, Vol. 17, No. 2, May 1964, 143-154.

Sykes, A. J. M. "The Effect of a Supervisory Training Course in Changing Supervisors' Perceptions and Expectations of the Role of Management." *Human Relations*, Vol. 15, No. 3, August 1962, 227-243.

Thistlethwaite, D. L., de Haan, H., and Kamenetzky, J. "The Effects of 'Directive' and 'Nondirective' Communication Procedures on Attitudes." *Journal of Abnormal and Social Psychology*, Vol. 51, No. 1, July 1955, 107-113.

Triandis, H. C. "Attitude Change Through Training in Industry." *Human Organization*, Vol. 17, No. 2, Summer 1958, 27-30.

Trites, D. K. "Adaptability Measures as Predictors of Performance Ratings." *Journal of Applied Psychology*, Vol. 44, No. 5, October 1960, 349-353.

Trumbo, D. A. "Individual and Group Correlatives of Attitudes Toward Work-Related Change." *Journal of Applied Psychology*, Vol. 45, No. 5, October 1961, 338-344.

Underwood, B. J., and Richardson, J. "Verbal Concept Learning as a Function of Instructions and Dominance Level." *Journal of Experimental Psychology*, Vol. 51, No. 4, April 1956, 229-238.

Underwood W. J. "Evaluation of Laboratory-Method Training." *Training Directors Journal*, Vol. 19, No. 5, May 1965, 34-40.

Vroom, V. H. *Work and Motivation*. New York: John Wiley & Sons, 1964.

Wallen, R. "Ego-Involvement as a Determinant of Selective Forgetting." *Journal of Abnormal and Social Psychology*, Vol. 37, No. 1, January 1942, 20-39.

Ward, C. D. "Ego-Involvement and the Absolute Judgment of Attitude Statements." *Journal of Personality and Social Psychology*, Vol. 2, No. 2, August 1965, 202-208.

Whittaker, J. O. "Attitude Change and Communication-Attitude Discrepancy." *Journal of Social Psychology*, Vol. 65, 1st half, February 1965, 141-147.

Wikstrom, W. S. *Developing Managerial Competence: Changing Concepts, Emerging Practices.* New York: The National Industrial Conference Board, 1964; reviewed by S. Levy, *Personnel Psychology*, Vol. 18, No. 1, Spring 1965, 127.

Wiora, A. P., and Trego, J. W. "An Experiment in Management Development." *Personnel*, Vol. 38, No. 3, May-June 1961, 25-30.

Wispe, L. G. "Evaluating Section Teaching Methods in the Introductory Course." *Journal of Educational Research*, Vol. 45, No. 3, November 1951, 161-186.

APPENDIX II

"Empiric Studies Concerned With Effects of Management
Development Efforts"

Andrews, K. R. "Reaction to University Development Programs." *Harvard Business Review*, Vol. 39, No. 3, May-June 1961, 116-134.

Asch, M. J. "Nondirective Teaching in Psychology: An Experimental Study." Psychological Monographs, Vol. 65, No. 4, 1951.

Bass, B. M. "Mood Changes During a Management Training Laboratory." *Journal of Applied Psychology*, Vol. 46, No. 5, October 1962, 361-364.

Bass, B. M. "Reactions to *Twelve Angry Men* as a Measure of Sensitivity Training." *Journal of Applied Psychology*, Vol. 46, No. 2, April 1962, 120-124.

Baxter, B., Taaffe, A. A., and Hughes, J. F. "A Training Evaluation Study." *Personnel Psychology*, Vol. 6, No. 4, Winter 1953, 403-417.

Bennett, W. E. "The Lecture as a Management Training Technique." *Personnel*, Vol. 32, No. 6, May 1956, 497-507.

Buchanan, P. C. "Evaluating the Effectiveness of Laboratory Training in Industry." Paper read at the American Management Association Seminar, New York, February 24-26, 1964.

Buchanan, P. C. "Evaluating the Results of Supervisory Training." *Personnel*, Vol. 33, No. 4, January 1957, 362-370.

Buchanan, P. C. "Factors Making for Effective Supervisory Training." *Personnel*, Vol. 34, No. 5, March-April 1958, 46-53.

Buchanan, P. C. "Testing the Validity of an Evaluation Program." *Personnel*, Vol. 34, No. 3, November-December 1957, 78-81.

Buchanan, P. C., and Brunstetter, P. H. "A Research Approach to Management Improvement." *Journal of the American Society of Training Directors*, (Part 1: "Description of the Program") Vol. 13, No. 1, January 1959, 9-18. (Part 2: "Methodology and Results of Evaluation") Vol. 13, No. 2, February 1959, 18-27.

Bunker, D. R. "Individual Applications of Laboratory Training." *Journal of Applied Behavior Science*, Vol. 1, No. 2, April-May-June 1965, 131-148.

Burke, R. L., and Bennis, W. G. "Changes in Perception of Self and Others during Human Relations Training." *Human Relations*, Vol. 14, No. 2, May 1961, 165-182.

Canter, R. R., Jr. "A Human Relations Training Program." *Journal of Applied Psychology*, Vol. 35, No. 1, February 1951, 38-45.

Carron, T. J. "Human Relations Training and Attitude Change: A Vector Analysis." *Personnel Psychology*, Vol. 17, No. 4, Winter 1964, 403-424.

Castle, P. F. C., and Garforth, F. I. de la P. "Selection, Training and Status of Supervisors: I. Selection." *Occupational Psychology*, Vol. 25, No. 2, April 1951, 109-123. "II. Training," Vol. 25, No. 3, July 1951, 166-180 (F. I. de la Garforth, H. F. Lock, and D. M. Sidney); "III. Status," Vol. 25, No. 4, 225-232 (I. F. Blain, P. F. C. Castle, J. D. Handyside, and D. M. Sidney).

Cohen, D., Whitmyre, J. W., and Funk, W. H. "Effect of Group Cohesiveness and Training upon Creative Thinking." *Journal of Applied Psychology*, Vol. 44, No. 5, October 1960, 319-322.

Dashiell, D. F. "Experimental Studies of the Influence of Social Situations on the Behavior of Individual Human Adults." C. Murchison, ed., *A Handbook of Social Psychology*. (Part 2.) Worcester, Massachusetts: Clark University Press, 1935, 1097-1158.

Davis, O. L., and Bowers, N. D. "Sensitivity Training in a Teacher Education Program: An Initial Attempt." *Peabody Journal of Education*, Vol. 39, No. 2, September 1961, 68-74.

Dearborn, D. C., and Simon, H. A. "Selective Perception: A Note on the Departmental Identifications of Executives." *Sociometry*, Vol. 21, No. 2, June 1958, 140-144.

DiVesta, F. J. "Instructor-Centered and Student-Centered Approaches in Teaching a Human Relations Course." *Journal of Applied Psychology*, Vol. 38, No. 5. October 1954, 329-335.

Filley, A. C., and Reighard, F. H. *A Preliminary Survey of Training Attitudes and Needs Among Actual and Potential Attendees at Management Institute Programs*. Madison: University of Wisconsin (Mimeo) November 1962.

Fleishman, E. A. "Leadership Climate, Human Relations Training and Supervisory Behavior." *Personnel Psychology*, Vol. 6, No. 2, Summer 1953, 205-222.

Fleishman, E. A., Harris, E. F., and Burtt, H. E. *Leadership and Supervision in Industry: An Evaluation of a Supervisory Training Program*. Columbus: The Ohio State University Press, 1955.

Goodacre, D. "Stimulating Improved Management." *Personnel Psychology*, Vol. 16, No. 2, Summer 1963, 133-143.

Gruenfeld, L. W. "Selection of Executives for a Training Program." *Personnel Psychology*, Vol. 14, No. 4, Winter 1960, 421-431.

Guetzkow, H., Forehand, G. A., and James, B. J. "An Evaluation of Educational Influence on Administrative Judgment." *Administrative Science Quarterly*, Vol. 6, No. 4, March 1962, 483-500.

Handyside, J. D. "An Experiment with Supervisory Training." London: National Institute of Industrial Psychology, Report No. 12, 1956.

Handyside, J. D. "The Effectiveness of Supervisory Training—A Survey of Recent Experimental Studies." *Personnel Management*, Vol. 38. No. 336, June 1956, 97-107.

Hanson, P. G., Morton, R. B., and Rothhaus, P. "The Fate of Role Stereotypes in Two Performance Appraisal Situations." *Personnel Psychology*, Vol. 16, No. 3, Autumn 1963, 269-280.

Hare, A. P. "Small Group Discussions with Participatory and Supervisory Leadership." *Journal of Abnormal and Social Psychology*, Vol. 48, No. 2, April 1953, 273-275.

Hariton, T. "Conditions Influencing the Effects of Training Foremen in New Human Relations Principles." Unpublished Ph.D. dissertation, University of Michigan, Ann Arbor, Michigan, 1951.

Harris, E. F., and Fleishman, E. A. "Human Relations Training and the Stability of Leadership Patterns." *Journal of Applied Psychology*, Vol. 39, No. 1, February 1955, 20-25.

House, R. J. "An Experiment in the Use of Management Training Standard." *Journal of the Academy of Management*, Vol. 5, No. 1, April 1962, 76-81.

House, R. J. "An Experiment in the Use of Selected Methods for Improving the Effectiveness of Communication Training for Management." Unpublished Ph.D. dissertation, The Ohio State University, Columbus, Ohio, 1960.

House, R. J., and Tosi, H. L., Jr. "An Experimental Evaluation of a Management Training Program." *Academy of Management Journal,* Vol. 6, No. 4, December 1963, 303-315.

Janis, I. L., and King, B. T. "The Influence of Role Playing on Opinion Change." *Journal of Abnormal and Social Psychology,* Vol. 49, No. 2, April 1954, 211-218.

Jones, D. H., and Carron, T. J. "Evaluation of a Reading Development Program for Scientists and Engineers." *Personnel Psychology,* Vol. 18, No. 3, Autumn 1965, 281-295.

Katzell, R. A. "Testing a Training Program in Human Relations." M. L. Blum, ed. *Readings in Experimental Industrial Psychology.* New York: Prentice-Hall, Inc., 1952, 64-70; and, *Personnel Psychology,* Vol. 1, No. 3, Autumn 1948, 319-329.

Kay, E., French, J. R. P., Jr., and Meyer, H. H. *A Study of Threat and Participation in an Industrial Performance Appraisal Program.* New York: General Electric Company, Behavioral Research Service, Management Development and Employee Relations Services, May 1962.

Kellejian, V. J., Brown, P., and Weschler, I. "The Impact of Interpersonal Relations on Ratings of Performance." *Public Personnel Review,* Vol. 14, No. 4, October 1953, 166-170.

Kernan, J. P. "The Effect of Laboratory Human Relations Training on Personality and Opinion Test Scores of Supervisory Engineers." Unpublished Ph.D. dissertation, New York University, New York, 1959.

Kipnis, D. "Some Determinants of Supervisory Esteem." *Personnel Psychology,* Vol. 13, No. 4, Winter 1960, 377-391.

Kirchner, W. K., and Reisberg, D. J. "Differences Between Better and Less-Effective Supervisors in Appraisal of Subordinates." *Personnel Psychology,* Vol. 15, No. 3, Autumn 1962, 295-302.

Klubeck, S., and Bass, B. M. "Differential Effects of Training on Persons of Different Leadership Status." *Human Relations,* Vol. 7, No. 1, February 1954, 59-72.

Lawsche, C. H., and Bolda, R. A. *Role Playing as an Industrial Leadership Training Technique.* LaFayette, Indiana: Organizational Research Center, Purdue University, 1958.

Lawsche, C. H., Bolda, R. A., and Brune, R. L. "Studies in Management Training Evaluation: II. The Effects of Exposure in Role Playing." *Journal of Applied Psychology,* Vol. 43, No. 5, October 1959, 287-292.

Lawsche, C. H., Brune, R. L., and Bolda, R. A. "What Supervisors Say About Role Playing." *Journal of the American Society of Training Directors,* Vol. 12, No. 8, August 1959, 3-7.

Levine, J., and Butler, J. "Lecture versus Group Discussion in Changing Behavior." *Journal of Applied Psychology,* Vol. 36, No. 1, February 1952, 29-33; and D. Cartwright and A. Zander, eds. *Group Dynamics: Research and Theory.* Evanston, Illinois: Row, Peterson & Company, 1960, 280-286.

Lewin, K. "Lecture Compared with Group Decision (Red Cross Groups)." In "Studies in Group Decision," D. Cartwright and A. Zander, eds. *Group Dynamics: Research and Theory.* Evanston, Illinois: Row, Peterson & Company, 1960, 287-291. (A condensation of "Frontiers in Group Dynamics," *Human Relations,* Vol. 1, No. 1, February 1947, 5-41.)

Lieberman, S. "The Relationship Between Attitudes and Roles: A Natural Field Experiment." Unpublished Ph.D. dissertation, University of Michigan, Ann Arbor, Michigan, 1954.

Mahoney, T. A., Jerdee, T. H., and Korman, A. "An Experimental Evaluation of Management Development." *Personnel Psychology*, Vol. 13, No. 1, Spring 1960, 81-98.

Mahoney, T. A., Jerdee, T. H., and Nash, A. N. "Predicting Managerial Effectiveness." *Personnel Psychology*, Vol. 13, No. 2, Summer 1960, 147-163.

Mahoney, T. A., Jerdee, T. H., and Nash, A. N. *The Identification of Management Potential: A Research Approach to Management Development*. Dubuque, Iowa: William C. Brown Company, 1961.

Mahoney, T. A., and Woods, R. G. "Developing an Appraisal Program through Action Research." *Personnel*, Vol. 38, No. 1, January-February 1961, 25-31.

Maier, N. R. F. "An Experimental Test of the Effect of Training on Discussion Leadership." *Human Relations*, Vol. 6, No. 2, May 1953, 161-173.

Maier, N. R. F. "The Quality of Group Decisions as Influenced by the Discussion Leader." *Human Relations*, Vol. 3, No. 2, June 1950, 155-174.

Maier, N. R. F., and Hoffman, L. R. "Using Trained 'Developmental' Discussion Leaders to Improve Further the Quality of Group Decisions." *Journal of Applied Psychology*, Vol. 44, No. 4, August 1960, 247-251.

Maier, N. R. F., Hoffman, L. R., and Lansky, L. M. "Human Relations Training as Manifested in an Interview Situation." *Personnel Psychology*, Vol. 13, No. 1, Spring 1960, 11-30.

Mann, F. C. "Studying and Creating Change: A Means to Understanding Social Organization." C. M. Arensberg *et al.*, eds., *Research in Industrial Human Relations*. New York: Harper, 1957, 146-167.

Mann, J. H., and Mann, C. H. "The Effect of Role Playing Experience on Self-Rating of Interpersonal Adjustment." *Group Psychotherapy*, Vol. 11, No. 1, March 1958, 27-32.

Mann, J. H., and Mann, C. H. "The Importance of Group Task in Producing Group-Member Personality and Behavior Changes." *Human Relations*, Vol. 12. No. 1, February 1959, 75-80.

Massey, J. C. "An Evaluation of Postal Service Carrier Training." *Journal of the American Society of Training Directors*, Vol. 11, No. 5, September-October 1957, 42-43.

McClelland, D. C. "Achievement Motivation Can Be Developed." *Harvard Business Review*, Vol. 43, No. 6, November-December 1965, 6-16, 20-24, 178.

McKay, Q. G. "The Impact of University Executive Development Programs on Participating Executives." Unpublished Ph.D. dissertation, Graduate School of Business Administration, Harvard University, Boston, 1961.

McKenney, J. L. "An Evaluation of a Business Game in an MBA Curriculum." *The Journal of Business*, Vol. 35, No. 3, July 1962, 278-286.

Meyer, H. H., and Walker, W. B. "A Study of Factors Relating to the Effectiveness of a Performance Appraisal Program." *Personnel Psychology*, Vol. 14, No. 3, Autumn 1961, 291-298.

Meyer, H. H., and Walker, W. B. "Need for Achievement and Risk Preferences as They Relate to Attitudes toward Reward Systems and Performance Appraisal in an Industrial Setting." *Journal of Applied Psychology*, Vol. 45, No. 4, August 1961, 251-256.

Miles, M. B. "Changes During and Following Laboratory Training: A Clinical Experimental Study." *Journal of Applied Behavioral Sciences*, Vol. 1, No. 3, July-August-September 1965, 215-242.

Miles, M. B. "Human Relations Training: Processes and Outcomes." *Journal of Counseling Psychology*, Vol. 7, No. 4, Winter 1960, 301-306.

Miner, J. B. "The Effect of a Course in Psychology on the Attitudes of Research and Development Supervisors." *Journal of Applied Psychology*, Vol. 44, No. 3, June 1960, 224-232.

Moon, C. G., and Hariton, T. "Evaluating an Appraisal and Feedback Training Program." *Personnel*, Vol. 35, No. 3, November-December 1958, 36-41.

Neel, R. G., and Dunn, R. E. "Predicting Success in Supervisory Training Programs by the Use of Psychological Tests." *Journal of Applied Psychology*, Vol. 44, No. 5, October 1960, 358-360.

Page, R. H., and McGinnies, E. "Comparison of Two Styles of Leadership in Small Group Discussion." *Journal of Applied Psychology*, Vol. 43, No. 4, August 1959, 240-245.

Papaloizos, A. "Personality and Success of Training in Human Relations." *Personnel Psychology*, Vol. 15, No. 4, Winter 1962, 423-428.

Preston, M. G., and Heintz, R. K. "Effects of Participatory versus Supervisory Leadership on Group Judgment." *Journal of Abnormal and Social Psychology*, Vol. 44, No. 3, July 1949, 344-355.

Pryer, M. W., and Bass, B. M. "Some Effects of Feedback on Behavior in Groups." *Sociometry*, Vol. 22, No. 1, March 1959, 56-63.

Sherman, H. *Reducing Grievances Through Supervisory Training*, E. E. Jennings, ed., Wisconsin Commerce Reports, Vol. 3, No. 4. Madison: Bureau of Business Research and Service, University of Wisconsin, 1952.

Smith, E. E., and Knight, S. S. "Effects of Feedback on Insight and Problem Solving Efficiency in Training Groups." *Journal of Applied Psychology*, Vol. 43, No. 3, June 1959, 209-211.

Spector, A. J. "Changes in Human Relations Attitudes." *Journal of Applied Psychology*, Vol. 42, No. 3, June 1958, 154-157.

Speroff, B. J. "Group Psychotherapy and Role Playing in Labor Relations: A Case Study." *Group Psychotherapy*, Vol. 13, No. 2, June 1960, 87-93.

Stroud, P. V. "Evaluating a Human Relations Training Program." *Personnel*, Vol. 36, No. 6, November-December 1959, 52-60.

Sykes, A. J. M. "A Study in Changing the Attitudes and Stereotypes of Industrial Workers." *Human Relations*, Vol. 17, No. 2, May 1964, 143-154.

Sykes, A. J. M. "The Effect of a Supervisory Training Course in Changing Supervisors' Perceptions and Expectations of the Role of Management." *Human Relations*, Vol. 15, No. 3, August 1962, 227-243.

Tarnopol, L., "Personality and Trainability: a Case Study." *Personnel*, Vol. 34, No. 3, November-December 1957, 82-89.

Tarnopol, L. "Personality and Trainability: a Case Study." *Personnel*, Vol. 34, No. 3, July-August 1957, 92-96.

Thistlethwaite, D. L., de Haan, H., and Kamenetzky, J. "The Effects of 'Directive' and 'Nondirective' Communication Procedures on Attitudes." *Journal of Abnormal and Social Psychology*, Vol. 51. No. 1, July 1955, 107-113.

Triandis, H. C. "Attitude Change through Training in Industry." *Human Organization*, Vol. 17, No. 2, Summer 1958, 27-30.

Trites, D. K. "Adaptability Measures as Predictors of Performance Ratings." *Journal of Applied Psychology*, Vol. 44, No. 5, October 1960, 349-353.

Underwood, W. J. "Evaluation of Laboratory-Method Training." *Training Directors Journal*, Vol. 19, No. 5, May 1965, 34-40.

Viteles, M. " 'Human Relations and the 'Humanities' in the Education of Business Leaders: Evaluation of a Program of Humanistic Studies for Executives." *Personnel Psychology*, Vol. 12, No. 1, Spring 1959, 1-28.

Vogels, David S., Jr. "An Evaluation of a Management Training Course." *Journal of the American Society of Training Directors,* Vol. 12, No. 1, January 1958, 44-51.

Wiora, A. P. and Trego, J. W. "An Experiment in Management Development." *Personnel,* Vol. 38, No. 3, May-June 1961, 25-30.